The Soul of

CREATIVITY

The Soul of CREATIVITY

Insights into the Creative Process

COMPILED AND EDITED BY
TONA PEARCE MYERS

NEW WORLD LIBRARY
NOVATO, CALIFORNIA

New World Library
14 Pamaron Way
Novato, California 94949

© 1999 Tona Pearce Myers

Cover design: Big Fish Books
Text design: Mary Ann Casler

Copyright Holders and Permissions Acknowledgements on page 211 are an extension of the copyright page.

All rights reserved. This book may not be reproduced in whole or in part without written permission from the publisher, except by a reviewer who may quote brief passages in a review; nor may any part of this book be reproduced, stored in a retrieval system, or transmitted in any form or by any means electronic, mechanical, photocopying, recording, or other, without written permission from the publisher.

Library of Congress Cataloging-in-Publication Data

The soul of creativity: insights into the creative process/
compiled and edited by Tona Pearce Myers.
p. cm.
Includes bibliographical references.
ISBN 1-57731-077-2 (alk. paper)
1. Creative ability. 2. Creative thinking. I. Myers, Tona Pearce, 1966–.
BF408.S584 1999
153.3'5—dc21 98-53426
CIP

First Printing April, 1999
Printed in Canada on acid-free paper
ISBN 1-57731-077-2
Distributed to the trade by Publishers Group West

10 9 8 7 6 5 4 3 2 1

Neither a lofty degree of intelligence nor imagination
nor both together go to the making of a genius.
Love, love, love — that is the soul of genius.

— Wolfgang Amadeus Mozart

Contents

Acknowledgments

I want to thank all the creative people contained within these pages and all the creative people within my life. Thank you also to the two favorite men in my life: my husband, Dutch, for teaching me that creativity exists in everyone, and my son, Taylor, for teaching me to slow down and give myself time to be creative, even while changing diapers. A special thanks to my family who helped me begin my creative life: Joan Skinner; Richard, Susan, Troy, Cathy, Tracy, and Rachel Pearce; George and Buddy Skinner; Charles Fox; and, most important, my grandmother, Beatrice Fox, who first showed me how to be creative in my own special way.

Thank you also to all the people who work with me at New World Library: Becky Benenate for believing that I could accomplish this project; Marc Allen for giving me the opportunity to accomplish it; Munro Magruder and Victoria Williams-Clarke who both contributed graciously; Jason Gardner for his constant support, help, and consideration; Mary Ann Casler for her thoughtful design and her friendship; Marjorie Conte for her energy and vitality; Gina Misiroglu for her enthusiasm; Dean Campbell for his dependability even in times of stress; Amy Garretson for her humor; Cathy Bodenmann for being my second mother; Stesha Norstrom for her careful proofreading; and Ryan Madden for turning my attention to most of the contributors in this collection many years before I even dreamed of the project.

I especially want to thank the contributors of this book for their wisdom, ideas, and inspiration. Even with their busy schedules they were willing to help me achieve this dream.

The Four Ways of Creativity

ANGELES ARRIEN

In the *Courage to Create,* psychoanalyst Rollo May states, "If you do not express your own original ideas, if you do not listen to your own being, you will have betrayed yourself."

In order to tap the uniquely creative in ourselves, it is important to honor the four ways of deep listening: intuition, perception, insight, and vision. Many indigenous cultures recognize that intuition is the source that sparks external seeing (perception), internal viewing (insight), and holistic seeing (vision). For these societies, paying attention to these modes of seeing is a way to honor the sacred and fire the creative fire. We extend respect to our creative, visionary process when we give voice to what we see or sense. *The Soul of Creativity* impels us to bring our voice and creativity into the world.

The Creative Spirit — the relentless power within us that constantly extends an invitation to be who we are — requires the capacity to be open to our authenticity, vision, and creativity. Writer Gertrude Stein tapped this archetype when she told emerging writers of her time, "You have to know what you want to get. But when you know that, let it take you. And if it seems to take you off the track, don't hold back, because perhaps that is instinctively where you want to be. And if you hold back and try to be always where you have been before, you will go dry."

The authors of *The Soul of Creativity* demonstrate the refusal to hold back or go dry, and they empower thousands to do the same.

Introduction

The Spirit of Creativity

TONA PEARCE MYERS

I started this book as a journey into my own creativity. Creative people inspire me, heal me, and take me on journeys into their own processes. But mainly they leave me in awe. For me, creativity is an intimidating word. Strong. Powerful. For those who reside in their creativity it means something closer to the soul, something of everyday life.

I discovered many things over the two years this book needed to come to fruition. Creativity, I discovered, can be strong and powerful, healing and deep, but it needn't be intimidating or scary. It can be found in the most seemingly unexpected places. It can be found in the way we wear our clothes, in the drawings of children, in speaking our truths. Most important, it can be found within each person's soul.

I learned a great deal from the contributors in this book. I realized that creativity isn't something found outside oneself — in classes or in workshops. Even within the most artistic acts, creativity is a matter of the soul. This book has brought me to the realization that creativity resides within me — an ordinary person.

Prior to working on this book, I was working on a project I believed to be both important and inspiring. I had just had a baby and found little time for my writing and artistic pursuits, let alone for myself. After completing my project and sending it out for publication, I received several rejection letters and felt stuck creatively. I hated that feeling. I wanted desperately to connect with that creative aspect seemingly so close to me before the birth of my son. I didn't want to be just a mother. I wanted to be an artist.

After a year of feeling depressed, I had a breakthrough. A friend showed me how most of my creativity was being channeled into parenting. To be an effective parent takes not only hard work, but to do it well it takes creativity and inspiring thought. I soon discovered that other people I talked with also made creative contributions to their lives, their work, and their families.

My depression began to lift and I took my project to my good friend and editor, Becky Benenate, who instead of rejecting my idea, encouraged me to expand it. She opened my eyes to the idea of going to the creative source and working with people in many artistic fields to contribute their thoughts as to what creativity is. I leapt at the chance to compile such a book. Not only would it help me, but it would help others realize that creativity resides all around us.

Right away I discovered that some people I thought of as artistic and creative didn't feel that way about themselves. How could that be? What is it about the word creative that makes so many people feel it doesn't exist within them? Some prospective contributors said "I'll give it a try" or "I'll do my best."

Others begged off saying, they weren't "really creative at all."

After talking with people, conducting interviews, and working with different ideas for over a year, the book began to take shape. It was born out of my quest for answers about my own creative spirit, questions such as, Where does creativity come from? Where does it reside? Is inspiration an internal voice of the soul or an external voice from God?

The contributors to this book struggle with these questions. They search their processes, their art, their hearts to share with us their views on creativity. This collection contains the wisdom of artists, sculptors, writers, anthropologists, actors — people of different ages and backgrounds all affirming the human capacity for soulful creating. Through their eyes we trace the path of creativity that leads from advice to healing, from the dark aspects of creativity to the creative process, all the time trusting intuition.

This journey begins where all journeys should: with inspiration. "Inspire" comes from the French word *inspirare,* meaning "to breathe." Inspiration breathes the creative soul into our minds and our hearts. It is the starting point of all creative acts. Without inspiration our creative acts would be lifeless — without the life that makes each act unique. Michelle Cassou, in her essay "Inside the Heartbeat of Creation," poetically takes us into her studio as she pursues a creative dream that has become more and more pressing: satisfying her longing to erase the fine line that separates creator and creation. The contributors in this section share what breathes life into their imagination and how they follow it through to their creative ends.

The journey continues with the creative encounter. Jean Shinoda Bolen, in her essay "Creativity: The Alchemy of Aphrodite," explains the interactions of soul and art through the Aphrodite consciousness. "[It is] . . . when the soul takes flight with the music and soars to rhapsodic heights one moment, and touches a deep chord the next. The interaction is spontaneous in form, yet its substance may be deep and moving. " Don Campbell, a classical musician and author, examines the link of listening as a means of tapping into our creative cycles. "The rhythms of walking, the pulses of our hearts, the utterances of pain, joy, and delight — all these natural patterns coupled with the natural sounds around us create the language of expression."

We are reminded that with all the light there must be a dark side within the heart of creativity. In this section we delve into the psyche in search of understanding the dark aspects of the creative soul. All creators have experienced the shadow side of creativity. Most artists struggle with it continuously throughout their lives. Eric Maisel gently guides us through the creator's painful secret: that failure comes more often than success. Jean Leidloff explains how to tame our beasts.

The journey continues from darkness to the healing force of creativity. Contributors in this section realize that even though the dark side exists it needn't destroy. In creating we bring forth life, and with life comes health. Every act of creating we complete brings life to our ideas, thoughts, and imagination, which fuels our existence even further. "Acts of discernment, insights regarding what is true for you, are ener-gized by the action of writing. You illuminate something previously known only in shadow. By writing, you give life to what matters, you give shape to what you know. You find your voice," explains poet John Fox in his essay, "Words from the Marrow." For Fox creativity can affect, heal, and even change our lives.

We end the journey by looking at creativity as spiritual practice or prayer. It needn't matter whether we believe cre-ativity is divinely inspired or that it comes from the internal recesses of our minds; it can still be enlightening. Many believe that in the act of creating there is a holiness — a spirituality. In "Brush with God — Creativity as Practice and Prayer," Adriana Díaz explains the lack of spirituality in her early training as a painter. "Neither church teachers nor art professors addressed the "I," that "I" longing to make its unique connection and con-tribution to God and Art. It took years for me to realize that my studies had been for the sake of training; putting heart and soul into the text of my work was the dimension of art one eventu-ally confronts alone. Now I had to go beyond being a trained person: I had to become an art-ist, one whose soul is expressed through the skills of one's craft."

Along this journey we are accompanied by the creative people who contributed to this book. Their words inspire, illu-minate, and uplift us. That they shared their ideas and thoughts with me so freely is a gift I honor and now give to you. My life is more inspired, more clear from having compiled and edited this project; I hope yours will be so, too. The goal of this book was not to explain to you what creativity is, but to help you find answers for yourselves. Everyone's truths may be slightly different because each truth is individual. In sharing these thoughts and ideas I hope to help others along their journey to the soul of their creativity.

Chapter 1

Brush with Inspiration

When I am, as it were, completely myself,
entirely alone, and of good cheer
— say, traveling in a carriage
or walking after a good meal —
it is on such occasions that my ideas flow best
and most abundantly.

— Wolfgang Amadeus Mozart

Inside the Heartbeat of Creation

MICHELLE CASSOU

I waited for spring recess, counting the days. The children would be off from school, and the painting studio would be closed. It would be deliciously empty. I would go in.

I had a project. My dream had become more and more pressing. I wanted to paint a painting as big as the studio, a painting that would cover the four walls, from floor to ceiling, and the door. I longed to be surrounded by my own creation, to be totally absorbed, to melt in it. I wanted to erase the line that separates creator and creation.

The studio, a small rectangular room maybe ten by twenty feet, has all its walls covered by soft boards where children pin their paper to paint on. The room has been multicolored by hundreds of painters when their brushes touched the borders of their paintings, leaving traces of colors. It has no windows except for one very small opening against the ceiling. It has no door, either, or so it seems, because the door is covered just like the walls, and when it is closed it seems to disappear. It is a sacred space. I was shocked one day to discover that fifteen years earlier it had been a meat freezer in the back of a butcher shop.

Life balances all extremes. Now it feels like a secret place, a womb where I can abandon myself, dive into my feelings with no fear or pressure from the world outside — as if it miraculously dissolved.

Empty and silent, the studio is pulling me into its vortex of creation. I feverishly cover the walls from top to bottom with large sheets of paper. I am getting ready to indulge in creation, to dive body and soul into its core, ready to answer the call of the mysterious unknown. I am going to paint the whole space around myself, to fill every inch of it with color and form.

I start to work on the right side and move from right to left, using ladders and stools, watching the images and colors reveal themselves under my passionate brush strokes. I have no plan. The miracle of spontaneity slips into the room and takes hold of me, guiding me. Exotic plants, multicolored birds, people of all colors — spirits are born, dancing with light and rhythm. My hand moves on its own. I watch with delight the fulfillment of my dream.

Time flies by. I paint for many days from morning till night, all by myself, inside my painting. I arrive just after dawn. It is always dark when I leave. I walk three blocks to the metro station, amazed at the world outside, mesmerized by Paris and its crowds of tired workers going home. The activity, the noise, the expressions on the faces fascinate me as the train carries me away, back to Charenton sur Seine, my home, where my young son is waiting for me. I know I won't have strength left or the desire to eat. I will just take my baby to bed with me, and we will cuddle. I will wrap my arms around him, his feet touching my folded knees, and our breath will mix. He will feel completely enveloped by me, relax, and then gently fall asleep.

✳

Now it is time to put the last stroke on the painting. I let myself slide all the way into it. I feel its full embrace. I stand in the most intimate fashion, in the closest possible way, at the center of my own passion. I am ecstatic. God's beauty fills me. My soul is full. Hidden in Paris, in a former meat freezer, I feel the greatest, the fullest lover's embrace.

That night as I walk out of the studio, my soul is drunk. I feel transparent as if the whole world could pass through me without touching me. Only an old instinct brings me home.

The next morning, pulled like a magnet I have to go back. I slowly and carefully open the door to the studio, holding my breath. The world of my painting is still standing in a vortex of energy. Joy and gratefulness burst in me. I softly walk to the center of the room, and suddenly I hear its heartbeat, the heartbeat of creation.

I stay there and listen. I do not know how much time has elapsed. But at a certain point, I wake back to the world and know that the next step is to take down the painting this very day and free the studio for the next painters.

Slowly, with great respect, I disassemble the immense

painting and stack the sheets. The painting disappears, one piece at a time, eaten by the powerful force of the void. Creation breathes in and out, comes and goes.

Nobody has seen my painting. I never looked at it again. Done for its own glory, its gift is still in me. Creation does not need anything added to it, no reward, no approval, no praise. Creation is a moment filled with spirit, a moment when the soul reaches far and brings back God's heart. Done for its own sake, it is free.

Life is movement, creation only a response. The pulse of existence goes on. In and out. No resistance. Creativity fills the moment. In and out. It is as sacred to take my work down as it is to let it unfold. In and out.

✴

Born in Hyers, France, MICHELLE CASSOU started to draw and paint when she was five years old. Her childhood was filled with dreams of inventing and creating. She created art with every available method and material, while innately refusing to engage with traditional structures. At 18, however, she reversed the direction of her work, and enrolled in traditional Parisian art classes, hoping to increase her power of expression. When this approach threatened to destroy the connection between her work and her feelings, she escaped by joining a free expression studio for children. It was there, from the children, that she discovered the magical force of spontaneous painting.

She spent more than three years painting with children. By painting freely, away from all traditional rules and concepts about art, she soon understood the amazing life-changing potential of creation. She discovered for herself the basic principle of making art: unrestricted choice and spontaneity. She reached what she calls the "point of no return," when creative expression moves to such a deepened level that one cannot imagine living without it.

This discovery immediately led to the desire to share it. Small groups soon gathered in her Paris home, where she transformed her bedroom into a painting studio. Through observation and experimentation, she started her lifelong search to understand the creative process.

In 1969, at the age of twenty-six, Michelle moved to Ottowa, Canada. She continued to paint while teaching her methods of "free expression" at the University of Ottowa. A few years later she moved to California, named her process the Painting Experience, and began teaching classes and workshops. Her art progressed intensely. She is now internationally known for her groundbreaking work of using painting as a tool for self-discovery, and for exploring the spiritual dimensions of the creative process.

Michelle has co-authored the book *Life, Paint and Passion: Reclaiming the Magic of Spontaneous Expression* out of her life's work and the thousands of paintings she has created. She is currently writing her second book, *Insights on the Creative Process,* which includes her latest discoveries on painting and creation. It will be available next year.

Her new video chronicles her painting history. In it, she describes how she discovered the freedom to paint and how anyone can tap the deeper energies of creation. She continues to paint and teach in the San Francisco Bay area. Michelle Cassou can be reached at The Painting Experience, 369-B #279 Third Street, San Rafael, CA 94901, (415) 459-4829. E-mail: cassouart@aol.com; Website: www.thepaintingexpe-rience.com.

Creativity and the Heart of Shamanism

HAL ZINA BENNETT, Ph.D.

*S*ome years ago my writing career had stalled. I'd sit down to write, but nothing would come. I was certain the well had run dry. It was disconcerting enough to experience a crumbling of my creative powers, but this was my livelihood. I had bills to pay, a family to support. How would we survive?

I consulted a psychotherapist, a psychic, and numerous friends. My therapist suggested I take a look at my relationships with my parents. My psychic explained I was transiting through a retrograde cycle. And my friends told me not to worry; things would work themselves out. No doubt there was some truth in all these answers, but being desperate I pursued a more radical counsel.

Throughout my adult life, I've had a spirit guide I call Awahakeewah. Being of good midwestern stock I tend to believe he is mostly the product of my consciousness, but I listen just the same, vacillating between trust and skepticism.

To contact Awahakeewah I simply visualize his presence. That day I instantly slipped into a blissful state. Awahakeewah immediately appeared in my mind's eye, quite put out with me — which didn't *exactly raise my spirits. Nevertheless, I mentally asked him for guidance. Why was I so blocked? Would my creative abilities return?*

Awahakeewah stared at me indifferently. As far as I could tell, my fate didn't seem terribly important to him. But then he said, "Each of us has a piece of that same Creative Force that made the universe. You are the steward of this part, but you do not own it. So get the hell out of its way!"

Frankly, I had hoped for a little sympathy. But Awahakeewah sat before me, poker faced, unmoved by my whining. I knew that if I were to make the most of his advice I had to let his words swirl for a while in my consciousness.

The first insight to seep through was the realization that creativity is never in short supply. To regain the power of creativity, I had only to get out of my own way. It worked, and today I need only Awahakeewah's gentle reminder to restore my abilities.

When I was in my twenties and thirties I read books about the creative process. Most argued that the creative person's impulse came from a need to compensate for early deprivations or wounds. They pointed to the imagery used by painters, writers, and musicians as evidence that these artists are motivated by early traumas in their lives, evidence that creativity is an effort to purge fundamental conflicts. But is not such purging a universal human impulse? Certainly it doesn't distinguish the creative person from the rest of humanity.

I'm convinced that the reason creative people draw from their own experiences is not just to purge their wounds but because their experiences are sources of compelling imagery and passion without which art would be vapid. Memories of wounds we've endured and ecstasies that have lifted our hearts are the very best resources we have for creating good stories, great paintings, and wonderful music that moves our very souls. We have only to think about Goya's war etchings, or Picasso's *Guernica*, or Stravinsky's *Rite of Spring*, or Charles Dickens's *Tale of Two Cities* to find evidence for this. It is, after all, our own experiences that we know best and that offer us access to the greatest depth of emotion and the most vivid imagery. However, it is something beyond that, the promptings of a demiurge — Plato saw it as the creator of the world, Gnostic philosophers saw it is an assistant to the Supreme Being in the act of creation — greater than ourselves, that motivates us to transform the images of our lives into forms that would uplift the human soul.

In intuitive-based cultures, shamans and artists have always shared similar roles. They stand outside their societies, at the same time providing a unique service, that of transforming everyday perceptions so their communities may move beyond their own wounds and human limitations. There is a demiurge embodied by all living creatures, a drive that constantly causes us to reach beyond ourselves. It is expressed at the most basic levels as an impulse in certain members of a species to reach beyond its present environment and develop new physical or mental attributes to thrive in that new place. It is found in the shaman who reflects on the present psychological, physical, or spiritual mind-sets, forging new ways of seeing: a new hunting route, a new way for a couple to speak to each other, or a new way for the community to relate to its neighbors.

The artist embodies the demiurge of transformation and change in a way that is very similar to, if not the same as, the shaman. They both recognize that most human limitations are found not in universal limits but in the limits of human perception. The hunters of early communities learned one hunting path to follow, and they followed it until there was no more game to be found there. Even after the route was no longer productive they continued to follow it because in their minds this was the only path available to them. It often took the shaman to "magically" produce a new map and to perform rituals that helped the hunters let go of their dependence on the old map and start following the new one.

Creative and shamanic processes are both transformers. They provide the magic that allows us to see the world afresh, to move outside the limitations dictated by our perceptions, to let go of at least a portion of our present mind-set. Most of us intuitively know there's a vast world beyond our human perceptions. We have had glimpses of something beyond, but we don't spend a lot of time there. Shamans and artists do, however. Something in their experiences encourages them to open doors into the world beyond perception. Although they don't escape the limitations of their perceptions for long, they do spend more time there than most people do.

The reality beyond human perception exists outside the perceptual capacities of our five senses. But through science and intuition we know that much occurs in the universe we cannot possibly perceive through our senses. Moreover, scientists tell us that a knowledge of what they observe beyond

the senses, made visible by electronic devices and research con-
trols, is ultimately limited by the mind's ability to know. We
have proof there is a greater truth out there that we cannot
know through the usual channels of human perception.
Creativity, intuition, and theology help us gain an understanding of what that is.

In the Bible, Paul the Apostle spoke of this phenomenon:
that which "Eye hath not seen, nor ear heard" (Cor. 2:9). And
he spoke of the ability to see beyond our limited perceptions:
"For now we see through a glass, darkly; but then face to face:
now I know in part; but then shall I know even as also I am
known" (Cor. 13:9–13).

So where does the creative process fit, and what is it that
shamans and creative folks have in common? The explanation
goes back to the magic that allows us, if only briefly, to see
beyond the limits of our perceptions. It lies in the magic that
allows us at least to see that what we've assumed to be truth is
only an illusion and that our lives need not be limited to that
aberration. The shaman does it with ritual; the writer does it by
skillfully immersing us in another world, in a way of seeing so
different from ours that we are forced to relax the grip on our
perceptions. Shaman and writer both create the magic that
allows us to change our minds. In intuition-based societies in
which shamans' special talents were valued, they often plied
their magic through storytelling. Dancing, drumming, chanting
around a fire, the shaman might also weave a story that transported spectators to a world beyond their everyday experience.
For a while they saw through other eyes and heard through

other ears. Although they would not permanently adopt the other way of seeing, the experience would help to create a space in their minds when perception itself was seen as illusion, thus freeing them to let in at least the possibility of a greater truth.

In that space created beyond the illusions of human perception, one may just discover those insights ordinarily described as belonging to the spiritual realm, concepts such as living in harmony with the natural order, feeling the presence of a force greater than oneself, or recognizing the power of love.

I've spoken of the shaman's magic. But what are the tricks the shaman uses, for these surely would allow us to step outside ourselves and let the creative force work through us. This is not to say that shaman and artist don't draw upon their passions, the experiences they filter through their limited perceptions. The power of our stories, our poems, chants, and rituals comes from the deep passions that we, too, have experienced in our wounds, our loves, our moments of ecstacy.

Although there's passion in the memories we maintain of our life experiences, the artist and shaman also have ways of standing outside them. It's a strangely contradictory stance: they're at once fully cognizant of the passions of their lives and fully aware they're part of a greater truth. For some it's the truth that humanity isn't just one person but a continuum of human life that stretches backward and forward through endless millennia. For others it's the truth that we are all temporal manifestations of a superior intelligence and a life force that is always and endlessly recreating itself. However artists experience the insight of a larger truth, it provides them a perspective I call "entranced detachment."

With entranced detachment we can be fully immersed in an emotion yet feel no need to act on it except to use it for creativity and, ultimately, transformation. In this peculiar state of being we stand at the threshold where we can let go of our sense of self-importance. We can let go of the passions we may feel for justice — to right some terrible wrong in our lives. We can let go of grief or the delicious pain of unrequited love. We can yield to our fear of death. And as we do, another world opens to us. We step into the world some call "the invisible reality." We step into the other side of life, the world beyond perception. And it is in this place, without the encumbrances of the physical body, that the imagination takes flight. Here the creative spirit is master. Here we discover a new perspective on our passions: we find we can mold them into characters and situations or draw the juice from them to tell a new story or create a new product, service, or program to help others find comfort and peace of mind.

Artists have much to learn from the shaman's art. Even beginning writers, for example, have a taste of the shamanic when they become so immersed in writing a poem, a scene for a novel, or a concept for a nonfiction work that the outside world fades away and they forget their physical surroundings. That is the basic trance state when shaman and artist step outside everyday reality and enter that place beyond — what Aldous Huxley called the "the doors of perception."

We already use many devices of illusion shamans have

known for so many centuries. But we often use them without either knowing their roots or knowing exactly what we are doing. Growing up in a culture that celebrates rational, much more than intuitive processes, we've come to look at the creative process in terms of craft and marketing. What is far more useful, I believe, is to reach back and capture the spirit that today hides within the more rational approach. What if we could, as creative people, learn those tricks, those sleights of hand, those trances and alchemical pranks that carried shaman and spectators beyond the limits of everyday perception? Those devices do indeed allow us to step outside ourselves and invite the creative demiurge to work through us.

Since that day when Awahakeewah counseled me, I have been more than ever convinced that the creative act has its roots in ancient shamanism. And if we're to reconnect with those roots, we need to go back and explore the shaman's path.

Living as we do in the scientific age, with its fierce faith that all events can and must be objectively verified or they do not deserve our attention, we've lost the meaning of magic in our lives. And in losing that I am convinced we diminish our lives and our spiritual potential. We block our own light, robbing ourselves of the magic that infuses every moment of life.

The creative artist, whether painter, sculptor, musician, scientist, or writer, cannot work without the magic. Of that I am convinced. We don't always know how to invoke the magic, and we're sometimes afraid to examine it too closely for fear that we may jinx it. But my experience has been that the better we know the magic the stronger and more accessible is our muse — and that's the state of mind through which we can transform the world.

✳

HAL ZINA BENNETT, PH.D., is the author of twenty-eight books, including two novels. His nonfiction books includes works on creativity, Earth-based spirituality, intuition, and healing. Titles include *Write from the Heart: Accessing the Power of Your Creativity* (Nataraj/New World Library, 1995) and *Spirit Circle: A Story of Adventure & Shamanic Revelation* (Tenacity Press, 1998). This essay is adapted from a book in progress.

Hal and his wife, Susan J. Sparrow, teach writing and creativity workshops throughout the United States. They can be contacted at (800) 738-6721, E-mail at halbooks@aol.com.

Saving the Cat

STEPHEN NACHMANOVITCH, PH.D.

> *Already at birth*
> *I was parted,*
> *not just from my mother —*
> *but body from mind,*
> *mind from its source —*
> *that's why I take up*
> *this soft blade*
> *of breath*
> *to cut me back into one.* *

Creativity is the soul expressing itself in speech, gesture, sound, color, movement, building, inventing. Before all else it is simply to be able to say something. That's one of the great mysteries in both art and everyday life: how something appears from nothing. After something is said, all kinds of tricks and techniques can be applied to make our work more artful. We can study Beethoven's crude, splotchy notebooks and see how he tested and turned his phrases, combined and

---

* Peter Levitt, *One Hundred Butterflies* (Seattle: Broken Moon Press, 1992).

split them, played all the combination and permutation games of art to make his statements more refined, eloquent, beautiful, energetic. Often the original ideas from which he developed his masterpieces of spiritual art were, in themselves, almost trivial or ridiculous. The important thing is to start someplace, anyplace. Then we can play with, refine, elaborate the original statement until it pleases us. Before the dance of inspiration and perspiration can begin, there must be some raw material, some spark of inciting energy.

In daily life, too, having the freedom and impulsiveness to *say something* is of the utmost value. How often has each of us kicked ourselves for not saying something at a certain moment, for being tongue-tied when faced with an unforeseen situation that offered the potential for conflict, love, danger, opportunity — tongue-tied because we could not formulate an appropriate statement, a single good word, only to realize later, too late, that it would have been far better to say anything rather than let the moment pass?

One evening many years ago in Washington, D.C., I was giving a little talk about this aspect of creativity. The conference was on the theme of inner knowing; among the participants were professionals in psychology, religion, anthropology, politics, and the arts. There were about fifty or sixty of us; we had just cleared away a lovely potluck dinner, and I sat in a chair giving this talk. That evening, and still today, I could think of no better example to stimulate a real encounter with the issue of "saying something" than an old Zen koan. A koan is a "public case," a story designed to put us in an excruciatingly uncomfortable position from which we may possibly jump into a deeper understanding of what it is to be human than can be expressed in ordinary words or thoughts. This koan concerns the master Nan-chuan (748–837) and his great student, Chao-chou, (778–897).*

Nan-chuan was head of a big monastery. One day, when Chao-chou happened to be gone on an errand, Nan-chuan walked into the main corridor and saw the monks of the eastern and western halls fighting over a cat. He seized the cat, suddenly produced a big knife that he brandished over the cat, and told his monks, "If you can speak, you can save the cat."

No one answered. So he cut the cat in two.

That evening Chao-chou returned to the monastery, and Nan-chuan told him about the cat. Chao-chou immediately took off his sandals and, placing them on his head, walked out.

Nan-chuan called after him, "If you had been there, you could have saved the cat."

This story is perhaps slightly easier to take than Abraham's being willing to kill Isaac, but it sounds pretty bad nonetheless. Our group became alarmed and agitated and began trying to find ways of getting past Nan-chuan actually killing the cat — the crudity and cruelty of it. Some vague childish laughter and commotion wafted from the back of the room as we turned our attention to the spectacle of a Buddhist master blithely killing a living creature, and then to the feelings of his slack-jawed, mute spectators. In those monks we can see, as in a mirror,

---

* This is one of the most discussed koans in the history of Zen and is retold in varying forms in all three of the most important koan collections: #14 in *The Gateless Gate*, #63 and #64 in the **Blue Cliff Record**, and #9 in the *Book of Serenity*, all assembled in China in the tenth through the thirteenth centuries.

each of us who has had the experience of seeing something we really care about snatched away, wiped out irrevocably because we didn't speak up in time. The crudity and cruelty are there, all right, right here today, whether a Zen master dedicated to attaining enlightenment for the sake of all sentient beings including animals did or did not actually cut a cat in two.

Nan-chuan seized the cat; what he then told the monks comes out differently in different versions of the koan: "If any of you can speak, you can save the cat." "If any of you can give an answer [question unspecified], you can save the cat." "If any of you can say a good word, you can save the cat." In Zen, a "good word," a "turning word," is not just any word but one that signals awakened awareness, a symptom of a mind that penetrates through to reality, free and clear. "If any of you can express *dharma,* I will save the cat." What kind of answer was he asking for: anything at all, or some creative breakthrough? Either way, there were no words to save the poor cat.

Perhaps the monks were arguing over who owned the cat, or perhaps they were using it as the butt of a philosophical disputation, such as whether or not a cat has the Buddha Nature. Perhaps the cat *is* mind, which Nan-chuan reveals as having been split, even before the story began. In any case, the monks' bickering, their dualistic either-or thinking, were as useful to them as a dead cat.

Who were these monks, these full-time professionals who could not utter a word in a moment of emergency? It is possible to be smart, holy, virtuous, busy, altruistic, artistic, or however activity we choose to characterize ourselves, and yet be totally unable to see what is in front of us and act decisively. Then whatever activity we undertake rides us rather than being our vehicle; it is like being worn by our shoes instead of wearing them. Chao-chou's response — to take that which is low and make it high, that which is beneath us and make it above us — demonstrates the totality of things, shows us that we can't cut that totality in two.

Chao-chou, the resourceful, the perceptive — why? Chao-chou's reply is wordless, absurd, but Nan-chuan qualified it as a good word. Perhaps Chao-chou might declare, with Isadora Duncan, "If I could say it I wouldn't have to dance it." Needless to say, if any of us, hearing of Chao-chou, were to imitate his gesture, that would not qualify as a good word at all, it would qualify as a robotic imitation — not, to use today's word, "creative."

If we borrow a straw sandal or two from psychoanalysis, we can see how saying something and saying a good word are not all that different from each other. One of Freud's greatest discoveries was free association, a simple and childish game: not looking for repressed memories, not looking deliberately for patterns or answers to life's conundrums, but allowing the "just anything" answers to take us someplace meaningful, as they inevitably will. For in the mind, as in the universe, there is nothing random. Free association means free of conscious purpose. No association is free from context and meaning, but it may reveal deep truth if it is free from conscious control. That is exactly what the Zen masters were looking for in a good word — not an answer calculated to be right in the listeners' ears or to produce an effect.

Nan-chuan and Chao-chou were masters of the instinctive, unpremeditated response to the situation before their eyes, like the Israelite woman who solved the same koan with such perfect clarity and even more profoundly than our Zen friends. Two women were arguing over possession of a baby, and King Solomon proposed to cut the baby in two. Solomon, like Nan-chuan, was ready to graphically play out the dispute to the point of cruel absurdity. In this case one of the disputants was the real mother, who shrieked that the king should give the baby to the other woman, anything so that it may live.*

The truth does not ride on a clever response, but on something immediate, irrational, torn directly from the soul. That's why the answer to a koan can't be figured out, but must arise from the soul like an instinctual cry of love or rage or whoopee. That answer is the soul of creativity. It arises, like the insights and ideas of small children, from an undivided mind.

I was sitting in a nice green easy chair telling this story when two four-year-old boys emerged from the dinner debris with a pile of styrofoam cups. They began galumphing into the space between the audience and me, having quickly zeroed in on the fact that this would be the quickest and easiest way to capture everyone's attention. They were having the most marvelous time!

_____

* Kings I (3:16)

Our group of gentle-spirited grownups, still a bit shocked and dismayed by the cruel image of cutting the cat in two, returned again to deliberating whether Nan-chuan really cut the cat or whether it was a symbolic gesture — a metaphor, a threat, an attention grabber, or just a pretense. Just as the discussion was beginning to take this painful turn, we had a harder and harder time hearing one another over the whooping and yelping of the boys. Do we make allowances for how in ancient and medieval times people played fast and loose with life and death in a way that would be very hard for modern people to take? Was the whole thing a fiction devised to teach through the tonic of shock? Someone pointed out that in European history the Thirty Years' War, with all its horrors, was fought over the question of whether, when Christians take Communion, they are actually eating the body and blood of Christ or whether it is "only" a metaphor. An animal rights activist began fuming. A priest and a psychologist were tossing around ways of comparing the cat to Christ, to the Buddha Mind, to unsullied instinctive consciousness caught in the gins and traps of civilization. Pretty soon our group of sixty souls was spiritedly arguing over the cat with perhaps the same vehemence as the monks of the eastern and western halls in Nan-chuan's monastery. And through it all came cutting, ever more knife-like, the wild whoops and shrieks of the two little boys.

Several people felt angry at Nan-chuan, Chao-chou, and the whole Zen tradition of teaching through these gnomic, absurd tales in which two masters engage in mental duels, called *mondos*, in which they show how clever they are at spitting out poetic images. Many of these koans feature nose pulling, name calling, smacking and slapping, teachers and students whacking one another upside the head, and other totally childish behavior. The approach strikes many people as just plain silly. Mind games.

In their *mondos*, those old Zen boys were indeed playing mind games, because as soon as mind takes on the form of serious, rigid, adult thought, we are stuck in a place from which creativity is not likely to come. The mind games are a form of volleying — an intensely social form of play in which people quest and probe one another in the hope of bringing out some insight, much as our group was now doing. This practice related to the old shamanic poetry/song contests of many tribal cultures and to its origins in child's play, where mind is kept ever fresh. In the *mondo* the play is not to win or lose, but to keep the ball going. If we could find a companion with whom we could keep the ball going for only three bounces, we would be blessed.

The theme that now had to come up in the discussion was how Chao-chou's behavior, as well as that of the author of the koan whose shocking story has by now managed to thoroughly wake us up, points us toward the trickster and the childlike elements of creativity. Creativity arises from the taproot of child's play. Creative solutions to insoluble problems often arise from spontaneous playfulness, from absurdity — and from conflict.

What we're aiming at in Zen, as in art, is to freshen the mind. Children have the freshest minds, but of course they also can be irritating, and some koans have the same qualities of being fresh and irritating and childish. It's almost as though those old Zen masters are little boys who will start wrestling in the mud any second; and perhaps, in the context of little boys, cutting the cat in two takes on a different flavor. I'm reminded that Picasso's art looks a great deal like children's art, except that it's not children's art. It's the art of someone who's profoundly trained and mature and yet had preserved the childlike part of himself and was able to reach back into that part from the vantage point of someone who had learned a great deal. Perhaps the Zen koans are childish in the same manner.

So there we were, twelve centuries after the fact, and still Nan-chuan was reciting to Chao-chou what had happened to the cat and Chao-chou put his slippers on top of his head and left. Nan-chuan said, "If you had been there, the cat would have been saved."

We were all sitting together working through the ins and outs of this story, but we couldn't quite hear each other because by now the two little boys were balancing the cups on top of their heads like tottering hats. Each boy was trying to knock the cup off the other's head. They were having an uproarious time! Our minds became divided between tracking the depths of the discussion and trying to shush the kids. My friend Abdul Aziz, with a thousand years of the subtlest Sufi mental training under his belt, was helplessly waving his hands and saying wise, fatherly things to them, like, "Boys, you have had your chance to play, now give the grownups a chance to play." But of course the boys didn't give a damn!

What sets Chao-chou and Nan-chuan apart from the rest? What was so creative about their absurd, childish acts that their seeming pranks have kept people meditating on them for centuries? A famous early Buddhist text tells us that a mark of enlightenment is to "attain the intuitive tolerance of the ultimate incomprehensibility of all things."* Through such tolerance, we become comfortable with the mysteries of life — mysteries being those truths that are immediately accessible through direct experience, but which cannot be known through heresay, theory, or rules of conduct.** From this comfort one is able, in a flash of intuitive certainty, to take decisive action at any moment.

If we can *see* the cat in every moment, so that we're always ready to save it, we are free. The story is not about how to free the cat, it is about how to free our minds. We began to recognize in this story the pondering, wondering, indecisive mind, sliced in half by dualism and possessive attachment before the story even began. The two boys were helping us overturn this split mind by demonstrating the directness of life itself, of our immaculate, whole, undivided mind . . . the two boys Chaochou and Nan-chuan, and the two boys in front of our eyes whom we were trying in vain to ignore so we could continue to ponder and wonder some more.

Intent, concentrated, and sincere, we were trying to listen to some funny old Zen story from the Tenth Century — but smack in the middle of the circle were two 4-year-old boys giggling and trying to knock cups off each other's heads. Unstoppable by the combined might of Moses, Jesus, Buddha,

---

* Robert A.F. Thurman, trans., *The Holy Teaching of Vimalakirti* (First Century) (Penn State, 1976).
** After Bertrand Russell gave the first talk about the Theory of Relativity at Cambridge, Alfred North Whitehead, rose "to thank Professor Russell for leaving the vast darkness of the subject unobscured."

and Muhammad. And the story we couldn't quite get through to was about Chao-chou putting his shoes on top of his head and heading out of the room.

Childhood's joy and spontaneity are not the same as enlightenment. What *was* Chao-chou's answer? Something unforeseeable and spontaneous, from the same evolutionary root as the kids with the cups on their heads, but also far beyond them. A good word is not the same as any word. Chao-chou's answer was the answer that cuts off the myriad streams of thought, like the Buddha's silence when asked certain questions, silence that woke people up. Such silence knows that to give pat answers is to limit the mind while inflating the mind into thinking it comprehends something it cannot possibly comprehend. Just as child's play is not the same as enlightenment, entertainment is not the same as art. The soul of creativity raises something from nothing; it comes decisively and clearly from left field and forces us to re-envision the whole mind-field. That, for example, is what the Impressionists did: why did anyone need one more really well-done perspective painting? All of a sudden someone comes along and changes the terms of the discussion. Decisively and clearly, Chao-chou puts those shoes on his head and strides out of the room to bring us closer to that intuitive tolerance of the ultimate incomprehensibility of all things. The soul of creativity.

How can we save the cat right now?

The illustration is by Sengai (1750-1837), "The Master and the Cat," ink on paper, 125.6 x 52.5 cm. Sengai's poem reads:

Cut one, cut all, the cat is not the only object.
Let them all be included,
The head monks of the two dormitories,
And even Wang (Nan-chuan) the old Master.

Peter Levitt provides the following variant of the epigram:

Zen this, Zen that,
Nan-chuan killed the kitty cat.
Chao-chou heard
And said, "That's that!"
Turned his shoe
Into a hat.

※

STEPHEN NACHMANOVITCH, PH.D., is a musician, author, computer artist, and educator. He studied at Harvard and the University of California at Santa Cruz where he earned a Ph.D. in the History of Consciousness. A student of Gregory Bateson, he has taught and lectured widely in the United States and abroad in the arts, the humanities, the social sciences, and particularly on the spiritual underpinnings of art. He has performed his own music internationally and has had numerous appearances on radio, television, and at music and theater festivals. He is the author of *Free Play: Improvisation in Life and Art* (Tarcher/Putnam, 1990) and is currently working on a book on creativity entitled *Genius & Magic,* from which this essay is taken.

The Natural Artistry of Dreams*

JILL MELLICK, PH.D.

The food of and for our soul is our imagination. When we do not feed our souls, we die a little. Denying ourselves this fertile inner realm of visual, auditory, and kinesthetic imagery disconnects us from our deepest, most sensitive, and most solid sense of who we truly are. Image, metaphor, symbol, and myth carry and translate messages between outer and inner worlds and among the domains of our inner world—personal, cultural, and archetypal. The arts can express, evoke, and mirror these inner images. By creating and contemplating simple art pieces, we can focus the energies of our personal and archetypal experiences.

For the Tewa Indians of New Mexico, artistic creativity is closer than breathing; it is the spirit of life itself moving endlessly through its cycles. Rina Swentzell of Santa Clara Pueblo explains that her people do not experience art as an activity separate from any other. The only word in Tewa that approximates the word art is *po-wa-ha*, which translates as "water-wind-breath," the creative force that moves through the waters

* Adapted from *The Natural Artistry of Dreams: Creative Ways to Bring the Wisdom of Dreams to Waking Life*, by permission of Conari Press, 1996.

and the earth. *Po-wa-ha* takes us back to the inexhaustible source of life itself; it connects us directly to life's creative energy. For the Tewa, art is a process, not a product. The real "product" of Tewa creativity is inner renewal, a sense of oneness with the life force.

All cultures value creativity and its expression through the arts. How sad, then, that so many of us carry unexamined, negative beliefs about our creativity, beliefs that disconnect us from our souls' first language. We believe that we need "talent," that product is all. We forget we have innate expressive capacities. We undervalue our individual capacities and needs to express ourselves creatively.

Creativity flows naturally in us as children. We take it for granted. It is as central to our childhood as is breathing. Outcome is not an issue. We don't ask ourselves, "Am I creative?" We just have fun and *are* creative. Unofficial initiation into adolescence usually includes obeying overt or covert constraints. Creative energies too often succumb to negative comparison, to performance demands, to unhelpful comments from well-meaning adults bound by limited vision. Creative expression ceases to be an integral part of daily life and eventually becomes "unnecessary," inaccessible. Our natural, creative self goes underground. We need to unearth and restore this buried treasure no matter how deeply it lies under the rubble of adaptive self-concept and behavior.

Creative expression pursued for the soul's sake needs to evolve through phases: intentional departure from ordinary awareness, inner journey into the imagination, return to ordinary awareness, and reflection on the journey. What distinguishes this kind of integrated creativity are the first and last phases. An artist who paints extraordinary material in a drugged stupor may be creative. However, the creativity is operating in a psychological vacuum and has not been welcomed into body or into consciousness. Complete loss of conscious interaction with the process of creativity diminishes our ability to harness these experiences and learn from them. We become prisoners in the strange realm of the gods. But, when we undertake creative pursuits consciously, we remain free travelers.

Dreams, creative expression, and soul are inseparable. They operate in an endless cycle. Each plays a crucial role in our inner life. Each needs, nourishes, and leads into another. Our natural creativity flourishes uncensored in our dreams. And our dreams use the language and structure of soul, a causal narrative logic that spirals in a timeless, spatially unbound world.

Many theorists assume that the dream's narrative structure can be fitted into a conventional Western narrative format — as though the structure is quite independent of its content, like a frame waiting for a painting or a survey, for answers. However, our dreams enact themselves in a different language and culture, which we can only partially understand. In *Woman Native Other*, Trinh Minh-ha reminds us that each culture tells stories in different ways. Each story has its innate structure. It is not only limiting but oppressive to retell one culture's story by forcing Western beginning-middle-end, cause-and-effect structure onto it so that it may make sense to us.

We often oppress our dreams the same way. We tend to separate our dreams' content from the organic, original "nonsensical" structure, and, to retell our dreams with logical coherence, we unthinkingly use the Western story structure. We have a dream experience. Then we reconstruct the dream in memory. Still later, we use words to represent the memory of the dream. The actual dream recedes further and further. Language reduces dream perception from several dimensions to linear descriptions of past, present, and future. So often we treat the words as though they were the dream. Sometimes, they are vitally connected to the life force of the dream. More often, though, they are a pale and flat record of a rich and timeless experience. But we are comfortable using this artistic medium (words) in one particular form (story) to express dreams.

Who said that all dreams are stories, and according to whose definition of "story"? Many dreams do resemble Western stories; in fact, our ways of storytelling probably influence certain dreams. We must be wary of the preconceptions we bring to our dreams from our daytime culture or from other cultures. Many dreams are not stories but natural plays, paintings, poems. Dreams prove us creative artists, natural poets capable of simile, metaphor, symbol, and sheer imagery unbound by the cognitive restrictions of waking life. Dreams prove us painters, sculptors, superb storytellers, mythmakers.

If we can allow the dream to be what it is rather than immediately adapting it to what it is not, we can allow the dream its structural integrity, which is probably best expressed through an art form more fluid than conventional story. The arts offer us other, more flexible ways than conventional story-telling to "re-member" and express dreams. We can express dreams in the art form that best suits them, in the art form whose structure is most akin to their innate structure.

By exploring our dreams through creative arts, we can reconnect with our innate capacity to creatively express our inner world, and we can widen the path to our souls. Moreover, by learning from other cultures' ways of structuring and expressing stories, dreams, images, and experiences, we can enrich our perceptions of and responses to our dreams. Free of the constraints of our answer-addicted, deterministic culture, we can open to new secrets, new themes, new ways of listening and attending, new ways of expressing our dreams.

We do not always need to fully understand or interpret dreams to receive their gifts to heart and soul. Rather, we can circumambulate them, let their images feed our imagination and lead us onward, just as a glimpse of ocean or lake renews and orients us on a long drive. Fine theatre and films leave images hovering in our awareness — the hand reaching across the car seat, the old letter being opened, the long shadow across the lawn. They also engender feelings that linger in the heart — inspiration, paradoxical whimsy, poignance. Even a film in an unfamiliar language can still touch something universal in the depths of the heart.

We need to let dreams paint themselves, dance themselves, sculpt themselves, begin at the end and end at the beginning, spiral in on themselves, meander without climax or major turning point. Perhaps then, when content and structure are seen as an indivisible whole, can we truly begin to appreciate the elegant sagacity of the dream.

If you are committed to exploring and expressing your dreams through the arts, there are several elements to which you may want to attend. Set aside time and place. Create a protected and private context. Release yourself temporarily from normal awareness, from personality boundaries. Do this with respect for the power of the dream and other imaginal material that may arise. With intent and context set, undertake your creative work with your dream. Allow material from deep within to surface; commune with the symbol or image. Your whole person — and its creative tools — becomes a vehicle for the symbol or image to move from unconsciousness to consciousness, just as it does for all creators. When you are ready to leave the inner realm, carefully allow the experience to come to a close and reenter normal awareness. A conscious completion and departure creates the distance from the experience, a distance you need for later reflection, insight, and integration.

When you consciously decide to undertake an inner journey to explore your dreams through simple creative artistic expression, do not set goals for how that journey will evolve or express itself. Let go of the need for particular outcomes, particularly those involving excellence, performance, or specific content. The mind provides apparent reasons and directions for what you are doing, but the soul provides the deeper reasons and directions. If you stay attached to the ostensible, you miss the real.

That momentary alignment of will and grace, of conscious

intent and unconscious energy, requires detachment from goal. In this kind of personal artwork, jettison any idea that you can help yourself or others by interpreting, praising, or criticizing. These have no more place than telling a mother that her child would look better with different-colored eyes. These kinds of creative pieces and experiences are only for being with. The only helpful response is to nourish the imagination and the piece by associating other images to it and noticing what feelings it evokes in you.

Overplanned dream art leaves little room for discovery. Discovering a repeated image, metaphor, or symbol is usually satisfying and energizing — no matter how shocking. We see how our unconscious has more insight, more coherence than we thought. Observe recurring images, ideas, colors, shapes, and textures without judgment. Do not evaluate. Experience.

The soul makes itself known to us through our unique mythology and calligraphy. Images nourish us and our journey. When contemplated they are wellsprings of wisdom. However, their efficacy and longevity lie in preserving some of their mystery. Take away all their mystery and we take away their power and life.

The more sense channels through which we absorb an experience, the more chance it has of being integrated into consciousness and the more deeply we are able to resonate with it. Moving from one medium to another is also crucial to free-flowing creative dreamwork. Choose media in which you are not competent. When you use a familiar medium, you run the risk of confining yourself to old habits and of becoming too self-critical. Each medium is a fine teacher, with subtle lessons for different times. I am unrepentently fickle when it comes to the arts. The fortunate thing about falling in love with media is that they are faithful. They hang around quietly until I am ready to be with them again. They don't lie about their capacities. They understand that I love them all. They accompany me into the unknown without criticism or praise.

On days when your self-judgment is criticizing everything, use your nondominant hand. This shift removes any possibility of your being invested in performance, competency, or outcome. It invites you into body awareness in the present: play first, work later! Warm up by using different media. Use the whole body when writing, painting, and sculpting; hands are just the final extension of a whole body response. Treat your completed work with respect. Date the piece, title it, and sign it. As soon as you have finished it, make notes on the back or on a separate page about your experience making it. Then photograph the piece. Leave work private, but visible to you and protected for contemplation. Images that emerge from deep in the unconscious sustain special energy for a long time. On their odd wings, they carry secret messages to personal awareness. Often it takes daily contemplation — even as you walk by them — to apprehend their messages. Choose places to leave your pieces out. Meditate on your work with eyes half-open in a still gaze. With your eyes open, then closed, play with the retinal patterns the lines and colors make.

A paradox of the inner path is that the more individualized and individuated our responses become to our experiences, the more universal they also seem to become. Think of poetry you have read or paintings you have seen: both reflect one person's experience of the world as well as a universal truth. When we receive, copy, or merge our experiences with others', we end up with stereotypical images; when we accept our uniqueness, we vitalize archetypal images.

Sharing our uniqueness with others provides them and us with ways to connect on a universal level. Talking about dream-work with trusted others reminds us of wider, deeper dimensions of human experience. Dream arts groups can function with as few as three people and as many as ten. When we talk simply and honestly about what we are learning from the creative explorations of our dreams, others also learn. Even when we describe something painful, talking about it with dignity and self-respect can be deeply healing for others as well as for us. The group's willingness to accept all experiences and the loving observation of each member's humanity allows all members to view themselves with dignity and to remember that pain and joy may be drawn from separate wells, but spring from a common artesian river. Leave a creative piece and its maker richer for exposure to your consciousness, not poorer. Constructive interpretation can often give a creator a momentary sense of being appreciated and understood. However, the long-term results of interpretation are less satisfactory; interpretation too often preserves the piece in intellectual formaldehyde when it could have led a long and vibrant life.

The Greek word "psyche" means "butterfly." It is also means "soul." Dreams give our souls wings. Pinning down our dreams with interpretations will tear the wings off the butterfly and kill it. We can put the dead butterfly under glass, study it, admire its uniqueness, and also let others admire (if they like butterflies). But it will never, never, never fly again.

The images from dreams are the exquisite patterns on the wings of the butterfly. Hold your dreams as you would hold a butterfly — in your open, quiet palms. Make sure none of the delicate wing dust brushes off onto clumsy hands. And feed your dreams by allowing them to express their wisdom through creative expression, freed from expectations of product or talent. In this way you will learn to hold your dream images so gently that they can still fly.

Dreams ask trustworthy questions, questions from our deepest selves. We can choose to have a passing acquaintance or a deep, long friendship with them. We can promise them we shall be with them, record them, sing them, dance them, laugh with and weep for them, draw them. If we are willing to make this covenant, we can then receive what comes from our dreams as unbidden gifts. Two separate, trusting people in a loving, conscious relationship cannot demand reciprocity. They can offer the other only the possibility of being with the other in ways that allow their best selves to fly together into an unknown, often moonless sky to be sustained by quiet air currents of acceptance.

Like lovers, all we can do for our dreams is promise to be there — with heart, soul, intellect, body, and discernment. If we can let go of demanding, we can begin to learn the dream's language of love.

✳

JILL MELLICK, PH.D., is a Jungian-oriented psychologist in private practice in Palo Alto, California. She is also a full professor and founder-
director of the Creative Expression doctoral studies program at the
Institute of Transpersonal Psychology. In addition to *The Natural Artistry
of Dreams* her most recent publications are *The Worlds of P'otsunu* (with
Jean Shutes) (University of New Mexico Press, 1996), the biography of
a Native American artist and elder; and *Coming Home to Myself* (with
Marion Woodman) (Conari, 1998). *The Natural Artistry of Dreams* introduces readers to more than forty ways to enhance creativity and understanding of dreams, nightmares, and dream series through painting,
poetry, myth, dramatic dialog, sculpture, fairytale, and movement.

Make It Real

SARK

*Y*our creativity is an immense force that is inside your every cell. Your creativity in action is so needed by the world and the people in it. No other person has your eccentric blend of ideas, attitudes, and perceptions. No one can see with your eyes. No matter how lumpy or faded or boring you feel, your creativity is of immeasurable value. There are treasures inside those lumps. Your creative thinking can save lives and souls and feed starving artists. The children need your creativity. You cannot say "I'm not very creative" until you have explored your soul and heart's gifts.

We are each born creative — then we forget our purpose, our mission. We believe our doubts and fears, and slowly we stop being creative as though it were a separate thing. Wake up! The light of your creative purpose glows brightly. Step into that light even if you're not sure what it is. When people ask what you do, reply, "I'm a creative spirit — I just came here to help." Move freely into your valuable creativity!

Creativity is here all the time. We're the ones who leave it.

We wait for the inspiration to start, yet it's really the other way around — first the action, then the inspiration. I'm almost never "in the mood" to create something. It never seems to be the right nuance of emotion or amount of time, or apathy drifts in and whispers things like "Why bother," "It won't look the way you want it to anyway," or just "Why?" Doing it anyway is just that. Create alongside the moods. Create when your laundry seems like the most exciting thing in your life.

When we put off beginning or completing a creative idea, we escape judgment and failure. When we procrastinate, we are often mentally or psychically rehearsing our steps and movements. There are gifts procrastination offers, however, and one of these is time. Sometimes we need time to rest or reflect or replenish our creative souls.

Our creative dreams so often stay in our heads, inside drawers, or in journals we stop reading. We forget the power of a real thing. When we give a creative dream form, shape, color, or design, it can travel without us to new lands. It then has its own life and is able to speak for itself. What will your "real thing" say? I often wondered how to get these treasures out of my head and into the world. It is much less about perfection and so much more about progress! When something is made real, it can help others to make real their creative dreams.

Creativity adores solitude. Provide quiet, creative time for yourself. It can first fit into the cracks of your life, and as you nurture it, it will expand into a glorious interior garden.

One of the most succulent spots I know of is my home, which I call the Magic Cottage. It used to be a toolshed and is only 180 square feet. There is no real furniture except for a loft bed, a hanging chair, and some big pillows. One wall is all windows, and there is a beamed ceiling and a wooden floor.

I write all my books lying on a futon beneath the loft bed, surrounded by books, cards, quotes, divinations, affirmations, magnifying glasses, bits of dyed string, special shells, sparkling rocks, photos, and cigar boxes full of fascinations. Shelves hold old journals, and here is what I wrote about the cottage when I moved in:

> The chimes have come fully alive here, their sounds follow me everywhere. Woodsmoke escorts me down the cobbled path, strewn with crackled leaves and bits of colored flower petals. The wind catches my rainbow banner and spanks it, reminding me of

Bahamian sailing adventures. Beyond the pale blue fence, I can feel the ocean. One candle lights my atmosphere, and illuminates the wooden beams on the ceiling and leads me to wonder who has loved here before me? There are creatures here, slugs in the bathroom, spiders spinning in corners.

A secretive mouse somewhere near the kitchen, a giant moth lying flat on the windowshade.There is a silence here, a polished gleaming quiet punctuated by foghorns from the sea. Rocks and shells and pieces of bark belong here. It is a ship, a Paris garret, an island hideaway, a fantasy treehouse. I am warm and safe and happy here. I am home at last.

This tiny cottage has helped me to make real eight books and many pieces of art. I feel truly safe and sheltered here, it is my creative laboratory. I hatch, cook, feed, dream, and burst into laughter and tears here.

I believe we need some space to make our creative dreams real. It can be in a journal, a bed, part of a room — anywhere that is yours and dedicated to your creative self. I send you the courage to make it real.

Describing the creative dream takes the creation one step further, but not so much further that you risk being judged, being found lacking, or even disliking it yourself. Describing it also uses up a precious energy: your creativity. If you explain your creative idea to every person, you are usually not working with the thing itself — it is not becoming real or visible, and

Your creative cycle is your transport

you can be drained by trying to explain it. In effect, you are not letting your creative dream have wings — and it needs wings! Making it real also gives dimension and explanation in a way words don't. Your vision is very much needed, and making it real is a way for us to experience you without meeting you.

Your creative dream can have so many more branches if it exists outside your head. Making it real also means that it may change shape and color as you work with it. As you create it, new possibilities will leap in, asking to be seen and considered. The real thing may change you. How can you know? Risk it all. Your real vision is immeasurably valuable, and I dare you to let it out. Let us all see what you have made real from your dreams and imagination. We are waiting to see. What is inside you right now that you can begin to make real?

SARK has captured the imagination and hearts of people around the world with her signature style of audacious wisdom and colorful artwork. Her eight book titles have over one million copies in print, she has sold more than three-quarter of a million posters and her bold, distinctive designs grave a successful line of gift products. Her appearances and book signings are standing-room-only "happenings," which seem to generate their own energy, and sales.

In 1993 SARK created Camp SARK, a thriving business that oversees all aspects of SARK'S publishing and licensing endeavors including: SARK'S Inspired Gift Collection of posters, cards, stationary, and calendars; *SARK's Magic Museletter*, a quarterly compilation of SARK'S imaginings and life; "The Inspiration Line," a 24-hour, call-in line (415) 546-3742 offering encouragement, which receives thousands of calls per month; and an increasing number of licensing agreements.

SARK lives in the Magic Cottage with her immensely inspiring black cat, Jupiter.

Two Dragonflies and a Volcano

ANN LINNEA

*D*riving down a road marked "primitive" on the map, I left behind pavement, fast-food stores, running water, and clean clothes. To the east, beyond the mountain, the large river, the irrigated fields, and the ranches with flowers and trees, there lay only sagebrush and brown grass and rocks as far as my eye could see. It was into this landscape that I purposefully turned my little white Subaru station wagon on an already hot July morning. It had been exactly one month since my forty-ninth birthday and the graduation of my oldest child from high school. It had been two months since the death of our beloved family dog, Willow. And it had been three months since I'd written one creative word. My well was dry, and I needed to tap back into the source.

I was leading two more carloads of women into a desert canyon for a seven-day vision quest-fasting experience. All totaled, nine women had spent a year preparing themselves physically and spiritually to make this journey. As one of the guides, my tasks would be to help with base camp details like safety, first aid, ceremonial participation, and other general hearth-keeping details. Their jobs would be to backpack in their belongings, choose remote spots, and immerse themselves in silence, prayer, and reflection for three of the seven days. Up one ridge and down the next the caravan of three cars moved until finally the one-lane rutted dirt road began its descent to our destination — a cottonwood-lined creek bottom about a thousand feet below the ridge.

Those who think the desert is a place consisting solely of shifting sand, sagebrush, and cactus do not know about desert canyon bottomlands. And that ignorance is probably just as well, for then these oases would be anything but solitary haunts for writers, mystics, and hermits. Even if this road had been paved, however, I doubt we'd have much company in July. Deserts in the heat of summer are not places for the uninitiated to be hiking in.

After parking our cars in the shade of some large cottonwoods, taking our snakebite kits, and saying our first group prayer, we donned backpacks and set off along the tiny, shrub-overgrown stream. Our intention was to walk until the stream created a spot deep enough to sit in, shady enough to sit beside, and flat and open enough to camp next to. Within thirty minutes we found such a haven. During the next two days the women forayed out to establish their individual quest sites, participated in numerous ceremonial and prayer circles, and then headed off for three days of solo fasting. During their absence my daily duties consisted of site checking, saying prayers, and maintaining our home base. That left me with a lot of time to simply rest and observe the life around me.

During the first of those three hot, hot days, while I sat on a rock under a small willow with my feet in the creek, a dragonfly landed on my knee. Its blue-and black-striped abdomen was thin and trim, perfectly streamlined for flying — probably the reason some call it a flying sewing needle. The iridescent, vertical blue and black striping continued past the abdomen to the thicker thorax. In this sturdier part of its seemingly frail body the dragonfly carried both flying and landing gear — not unlike the midsection of a 747, which expands to house wings, wheels, and a second passenger deck. My visitor's lacy, double-paired translucent wings didn't look strong enough to support its flight. But then, I'd seen the apparently sturdy thirty-foot metal wing of a 747 flex in wind gusts, so I knew my eyes were poor judges of aviation fitness.

But what most captured my attention were its huge eyes. Its thorax merged with a head that seemed to be nothing but two huge eyes! And though its dainty, six-footed landing gear had settled on my knee with head facing away from me, our eyes were still looking at each other. Each of its immense eyes contained many, many smaller eyes — like marbles in a glass jar, they enabled it to see forward, backward, and sideways in both directions. And like the earliest planes, this cockpit had a 360-degree view. The dragonfly and I settled down to keeping each other company in our shady hiding place, but we had only become acquainted when its brown, drab mate flew in, landed on top of it, and began copulating. I felt almost embarrassed by this brazen familiarity, but was so mesmerized by the audacity of it all that I held perfectly still.

My eyes moved back and forth between the complex eyes of the brown stranger and my blue dragonfly. The only other sensory input I was aware of was "cool" coming from my creek-bound feet. And that's all I was in the moment — a pair of eyes and a pair of feet. The complete attention to external sensory input and lack of attention to internal thought was as refreshing on this inferno of a day as a cool puff of wind or a glass of ice water. I didn't have to do anything — not write cards to those bringing flowers to Willow's grave or gifts to my son's graduation, not prepare food or vacuum or weed the garden, not make one more marketing call for our business. Watching two dragonflies was enough.

Suddenly I felt a tickling on my toes and jerked them out of the water in surprise. This, of course, propelled the enmeshed duo to find a more stable repose. My attention turned to the source of my next diversion from the heat. Three minnows — all about the size of my thumb — swam upstream in a line, delicate brown bodies and tails undulating in the current. Were they the culprits? Slowly I put my foot back into the creek, which was barely deep enough in this spot to keep fish or me wet. Quickly they swam over to assess the possibility of a gargantuan meal. I kept my foot still as long as I could stand the nibbling, then spooked them by wriggling my toes.

Although sitting nearly perfectly still — exercising nothing except my eyeballs and occasionally rearranging my sitting position — I was sweating rivulets of water from under my arms and breasts and the fold of skin that marks my soft, middle-aged belly. I guessed the temperature to be well over 100°F.

I drank five gulps of my filtered stream water and shifted my gaze beyond my immediate concerns.

Across the creek two red-shafted flickers were chattering as they made trip after trip from a willow thicket up to a large hole in an old cottonwood. Although I couldn't see any heads peeking out of the cavity, it was clear that their actions were those of harried parents with hungry youngsters. Suddenly, a loud chatter erupted in an alder thicket beneath the old nesting tree. I was sure the noise was coming from one bird, but the variations of tones and cheeps could have come from about fifteen species. When the dark head and bright chest of the yellow-breasted chat emerged briefly on top of one alder, I chuckled. It reminded me of the time sixteen years ago when my son and I had been strolling hand in hand down a desert wash and had spent the better part of a morning listening and straining to see this noisy, elusive warbler. My mind felt so free and easy — sauntering from one observation to the next, unfettered by anything more pressing than my discomfort in the heat. It was exactly this ease I had sought — for only when my mind is rested and curious can I stand on the threshold of creativity.

In my other life as mother, partner, and business owner, I forget how to saunter. The TV news, the office computer, the home answering machine, the errands, even the conversations I have with people demand quickness, cleverness, precision. The combination of pace and constant bombardment propels me away from the quieter rhythms of creativity. Only a return to the grand, soothing, often subtle rhythms of nature — the rising and setting of the sun, the whisper of wind in the trees,

the solidness of a mountain, the eternal motion of the sea —
can draw me back to the well of my creativity.

My thoughts went next to the questers, who were all within a mile radius of where I now sat. Where were they on this
hottest of days in this hottest of months? Were others of them
sitting with their feet in the creek, or were they sleeping in the
shade of their simple shelters? Usually when I seek nature to
inspire me, I am alone. And though sitting here alone, I felt
companioned in my intention to strip down past the familiarity of routines and schedules and expectations of others to find
the strength of the central storage system of my life.

My eyes moved to the dry, rocky slope above the cottonwood where several huge ponderosa pines stood. For me these
are the sentinels of desert canyons. Growing well above the
lush bottomlands, these hundred-foot-plus guardians reach
skyward almost as if they are craning to get a view of the high
plateau above. Where and how their roots are able to take hold
in the treacherous, baked scree slopes is beyond my understanding. Yet, not only do they take hold and manage the engineering feat of supporting their huge vertical structures, but
also they are able to ferret out scarce reservoirs of water during
months with no rain. Distinguished by their three-needle bun-
dles and cinnamon-colored, platy bark, these denizens of dry
places contain the same plumbing systems that enables all tall
trees to move water from the ground: through microscopic
tubes of some 100 feet up to their thin, green, food-producing
needles. If only the questers and I had such coping mecha-
nisms! We carry water filters and plastic storage bottles and

worry about surviving for just three days because we do not know how to make food from air and water and our storage systems have shallow reservoirs.

To my eye these pines are not stressed by the heat — the long needles were all full and green. The trees appeared as healthy as any that grow around my home, where rains are abundant. How could this be? How is nature equipped to deal with stress in ways that I'm not? How might I learn to find sustenance where there seems to be none? I have studied trees for a long time. I believe they can teach me how to tap universal reserves so that I might learn to stand as a sentinel regardless of whether I'm living through abundance or drought. And I also know that I need years more in their tutelage to learn these lessons.

Upslope from the towering pines were row after row of basalt columns, thin, stern-face guardian columns of stone soldiers created by molten magma from a Mt. Rainier eruption more than 10,000 years ago. I could see wide deltas of reddish gray rock — the result of eons of eroding of these seemingly permanent creations.

The heat of creation that formed this canyon happened so long ago, yet it was here now, too, descending like the hand of an invisible giant determined to immobilize and capture me. I found it hard to breathe, to take in any more of the heat. Then suddenly, I felt my own fire rising, bubbling, spewing forth. And I knew I must write — not should or could or will — but must.

Words came spitting onto the page like rocks ejected from a great crater. There was no regularity to them, but rather a sense that they were a precursor of bigger things to come. For two hours the words came. And the next day in the fire of another midday heat marathon they came again, covered page after page — a magma laying the foundation of a story. In the days that followed there was a weathering of those flows, the gentle edits of the passage of time. And when our quest ended, I had laid an important legacy in words — had followed the guidance of the great volcano of my home state of Washington, which leaves its legacy in form and shape. I had connected to the flow of a source larger than my own small life and its habits. Once again the natural world had returned me to the well-spring of my creativity.

✳

ANN LINNEA holds a B.S. from Iowa State University and an M.A. from the University of Idaho. Her writing career began in the 1970s when she wrote a hiking and skiing guide during her years as a U.S. Forest Service naturalist. She coauthored the award-winning *Teaching Kids to Love the Earth* (Pfeifer-Hamilton, 1991). Her most recent book is *Deep Water Passage, A Spiritual Journey at MidLife* (Little Brown, 1995; Pocket Books, 1997), the story of her midlife rite of passage — circumnavigating Lake Superior by sea kayak in the coldest, wettest summer in 100 years. Linnea has been a naturalist and teacher of outdoor skills for three decades. For the past fifteen years she has been dedicated to helping people build bridges between their lives and the sacred presence of the natural world. She is available for speaking engagements, seminars, training, and consultation. Contact her through PeerSpirit, P.O. Box 550, Langley, WA 98260.

Chapter 2

The Creative Encounter

Entering more deeply into the creative process,
the artist begins to receive spontaneous gifts:
signs and meanings suggest themselves "from nowhere" —
forms previously unimagined, new themes or motifs
that seem remarkably fertile. The working faculties
and the companion self have come to life,
shedding seeds with abandon and generosity. . . .
A degree of spontaneous ability has made itself known,
always a gift however much one reaches for it.

— Roger Lispey

Creativity:
The Alchemy of Aphrodite

JEAN SHINODA BOLEN, M.D.

The ability of Aphrodite — the Greek goddess of love and beauty — to bring a work of art to life is told in the myth of Pygmalion the sculptor who fell in love with his statue and prayed to Aphrodite that he might find a woman to love as beautiful as his statue. Aphrodite heard his prayer and granted his wish. Thus, when Pygmalion went home and kissed the statue, it came to life. Aphrodite had transformed the cold marble into the warm and lovely Galatea.

This story inspired the Pygmalion effect, which described how under-achieving students lived up or down to their teachers expectations. When one person sees the potential beauty or talent or ability in another and draws it out, the Pygmalion effect occurs. In *Goddesses in Everywoman*, I called Aphrodite the "Alchemical Goddess" because of the transformative effect that characterizes this archetype. Aphrodite is an essential element in the creative process. When we are creative, we are absorbed, fascinated, and involved in an interaction with our medium, which can be people as well as canvas and paint, the page or screen on which we write, the plants and earth that we garden, or the materials in the laboratory or studio with which we work. In the creative encounter there is an absorbing, unpossessive love and a sense that we are engaged in soul work.

The mind, vision, or hand of the artist in any medium is energized and inspired by Aphrodite. That is to say, the work is imbued with life — and soul. When we love what we do, we see beauty in it, for beauty is in the eye (or soul) of the beholder. Love and beauty go together whenever Aphrodite's influence is felt. Divine grace is in the flow of creative work. Although it grows out of the talent and skill of the artist and the inherent qualities of the medium, if it is inspired work Aphrodite is an invisible third presence.

APHRODITE CONSCIOUSNESS AND JUNGIAN ANALYSIS

Whenever we shift into what I categorize as Aphrodite consciousness (in contrast to diffuse awareness or focused consciousness) we are in a quality of consciousness in which we focus on and are receptive to what is in our field of attentiveness, as if what we are seeing is illuminated by a special light. What we behold has an impact on us, and we are affected by the experience. For example, the theater lighting enhances the performance on stage and darkens everything extraneous. The stage is set for us to be emotionally transported by a symphony, or be moved by a play, or by the words of a speaker. Feelings, sense impressions, and memories are drawn out of us in response to what we see and hear. In turn, those onstage can become inspired by an audience, energized by the rapport they sense being directed toward them. It is an I-thou interchange, a meeting at a soul level, at such times.

My conception of Aphrodite consciousness began in observing the process of analysis, in comparing notes with artists and writers, and in feeling how similar psychotherapy, painting, and writing are. In an analytic session several processes go on simultaneously. I am absorbed in listening to my patient, who has my rapt attention and compassion. At the same time my mind is active, mentally associating to what I am hearing. Things I already know about the person come to mind — perhaps a dream, or knowledge about the family, an incident, or current events in the person's life that may have a bearing. Sometimes an image comes up or a metaphor suggests itself. Or, I may have an emotional response, whether to the material or to the way it's expressed, which I note. My mind is actively working, but in a receptive way, stimulated by my absorption in the other person.

What I respond to during my analytic session is like one part of a large mosaic, an important detail in a much larger, only partially completed picture of the person in therapy with me, who is also someone with whom I am involved in a reciprocal process. If we are engaged in transformative work, an emotional field is generated between us powerful enough to touch us both. As Jung noted, analysis involves the totality of both personalities, the conscious attitudes and unconscious elements in both the doctor and the patient. If one person, the patient, is to be affected by the work, the doctor must be also.

He wrote, *"For two personalities to meet is like mixing two different chemical substances: if there is any combination at all, both are transformed."**

In doing therapy I gradually became aware that, in addition to the interactive, receptive Aphrodite consciousness that facilitates change and growth, I also had to keep an optimal emotional distance. If I feel too much or am too closely identified with my patient, I lack some essential objectivity. If I am too distant and lack love for my patient, I lose a crucial empathic connection, without which there isn't enough transformative energy to bring about deeper change.

APHRODITE CONSCIOUSNESS, CREATIVE SOLITUDE, AND CREATIVE COMMUNICATION

Aphrodite consciousness is present in all creative work, including that done in solitude. The dialog is then between the person and the work, from which something new emerges. For example, observe the process when painters are engaged with paint and canvas. An absorbed interchange occurs. They react or are receptive to the creative accidents of paint and brush. They may initiate actively with bold stroke, nuance, or color; and then, seeing what happens, they respond. It is an interaction: spontaneity combined with skill. It is an interplay between artist and canvas, a nonverbal creative dialog out of which something new is created.

Moreover, although painters focus on the details in front of them, they also hold an awareness of the whole canvas in their

---

* C.G. Jung, "Problems of Modern Psychotherapy," *Collected Works*, vol. 16 (Bollingen Series, 1966).

consciousness. At times they step back and objectively see what they have been so subjectively involved in creating. They are absorbed, involved — and also detached and objective.

In both good communication and creative process, there is an interaction at the soul level. Conversation, for example, can be banal, meaningless, wounding — or it can be an art form, as spontaneous, moving, and wonderful as musical improvisation or jam sessions, when the soul takes flight with the music and soars to rhapsodic heights one moment and touches a deep chord the next. The interaction is spontaneous in form, yet its substance may be deep and moving. Those conversing feel excitement and discovery as each sparks a response in the other. They mutually experience Aphrodite consciousness, which provides the energy field or backdrop for communication or creativity to happen. Where the music will go or how the conversation will evolve is not known or planned for at the start. Discovery — the birth of something new — is the key element in creativity and such communication.

Whenever Aphrodite consciousness is present, energy is generated: lovers glow with well-being and heightened energy, conversation sparkles, thoughts and feelings are stimulated. When two people truly meet each other, both are energized by Aphrodite and feel more vitality than before, regardless of the content — which, in therapy, can be painful material. When work becomes invigorating rather than draining, creativity is involved. Absorbed by whom we are with or by what we are doing — which is to be in Aphrodite's presence — we lose track of time.

CREATIVITY, KAIROS, AND MEANING

Whenever we are engaged in creativity, our experience of time is what the Greeks meant by *kairos,* or "participatory time." Absorption in the moment is total, there is no clock watching, often there is little or no sense of time passing. Whenever we are so absorbed, the soul is engaged and nourished by what we are doing. Invariably, there is a sense of being ourselves and of unselfconsciousness. Whatever we may be doing, however difficult or challenging it may seem, it is play, or, as Joseph Campbell expressed it, we are following our bliss.

Work that draws upon our creativity and intelligence, that takes skills we have honed with practice, uses us. It feels as if we are in service to the divinity in us or that we are living from our archetypal depths. We are then living our personal myth, and as we do, life has meaning to us.

There are many expressions of creativity; most are not recognized as art and yet they are. In each of us there is a poet or artist who takes pleasure in making something beautiful or expresses something that is truly us. Creative soul qualities are, however, not just in the expression of creativity, but in the appreciation of it as well. Creativity is interactive and art is alchemical; its power is in its capacity to affect and transform the artist and the audience.

LIMINALITY AND APHRODITE

"Liminality" comes from the Latin word meaning "threshold." Liminal experiences are threshold experiences that occur at the boundaries or growing edges of the psyche. This is where visible and invisible worlds overlap — the land of the soul. This is where individual consciousness and the collective unconscious meet and merge — where creative ideas and work are birthed. This is when we are in transition ourselves, neither who we used to be nor who we are becoming, and therefore are involved in our ongoing creation.

There is essential liminality about creativity as there is about any experience that is touched by Aphrodite and that has the ability to change us from within. If we continue to grow psychologically, spiritually, and humanly (in contrast to being inflexible, rigid, or bound by tradition), we ourselves are a creative work in process. When we recognize this, we will know that what we do with our lives is our magnum opus, our most important creative work.

✳

JEAN SHINODA BOLEN, M.D. is an internationally known Jungian analyst and author of *Goddesses in Everywoman: A New Psychology of Being* (HarperCollins, 1984); and *Gods in Everyman* (HarperCollins, 1990); *The Tao of Psychology* (Harper SanFrancisco, 1979); *Ring of Power* (Nicholas-Hays, 1999); and *Close to the Bone: Life-Threatening Illness and the Search for Meaning* (Simon and Schuster, 1998). She is a clinical professor of psychiatry at the University of California Medical Center in San Francisco, a Fellow of the American Psychiatric Association and the American Academy of Psychoanalysis, and a former member of the board of trustees of Ms. Foundation for Women and of the International Transpersonal Association. She had been involved in Healing Journeys: Cancer as a Turning Point conferences and was in two acclaimed documentaries: the Canadian Film Board's *Goddess*

Remembered and the Academy Award-winning antinuclear film, *Women — For America, For the World.* Two of her forthcoming books are *The Millionth Circle: How to Change Ourselves and the World* and *Goddesses in Older Women.* Her website is www.jungindex.net/bolen.

The Practice of Creativity in the Workplace

SHAUN MCNIFF, Ph.D.

As a young artist T.S. Eliot worked during the day as a banker and wrote poetry at night. Many artists faced with the demands of earning a living have operated within similar schedules, making clear divisions between creative expression and employment. As an artist who has spent my life in various jobs, I have always focused on the integration of work and creative activity. My art and my work are inseparable. I don't wish to imply that integration is better than the compartmentalized approach. It's just a way that has many benefits for both creative expression and the workplace. When creative expression is viewed exclusively as something done by artists working alone and separate from the world, life suffers.

My work with the creative process has always focused on how the medicines and transformations of art can benefit every sector of daily life, from the personal to the public. I am inspired by artists like Tyree Guyton, who transform environments into works of art. Guyton's Heidelberg Project makes an economically impoverished Detroit street into an affirmation of the creative spirit. The vision of Guyton's project together with the energy applied to its realization results in a wondrous environment that significantly augments one's perception of art. Guyton creates with his immediate environment. He starts with what he has — both physically and emotionally. He doesn't reach beyond himself, but takes something that is viewed as debased and turns it into an ambitious artwork.

If artistic creations emerge from our lives and the ways in which we see the world, then it seems useful to engage the workplace as a source of creative subject matter and energy. The job is the place where most of us spend time and expend effort each day. It is the world that we inhabit, and I believe we can make it better and more satisfying through the conscious use of the creative process. This essay, then, suggests ways of dealing with the question of how to achieve an integration of art and work.

I am asked, "How do I do this? My job demands all my time and energy. I am not an artist."

When people say they are not creative or talented, I respond by asking them to examine where and when that point of view originated. Because the creative process is based on how a person perceives the world, the best place to begin is with attitudes and perceptions. I trust that any person with a creative vision can take advantage of life situations and make them into art.

THE TECHNIQUE

My technique for teaching creative perception begins with identifying something a person finds worthless: a spot on the floor, a scrap of paper, a quick scribble with a pencil.

When the person says to me, "That's nothing," I say, "Listen to the voice that is judging and dismissing this thing in front of us. Who is speaking? From where does this voice originate?"

We must first become aware of our automatic tendencies to dismiss things and block opportunities for creative perception. I find it helps people to view how these dismissals uphold the way things are now. Apparently worthless and peripheral things are sources of innovation and insight when approached with a creative eye.

Engaging the worthless scrap of paper as a living thing expands our spectrum of perception by taking us out of our habitual ways of viewing life. I may ask, "What does the scrap of paper have to say about being called 'nothing'?" Invariably, personifying what is perceived to be worthless expands the range of possibilities.

The most important move in reframing our perceptions involves giving value to what is first seen as worthless: "Can you make the scrap of paper the most important thing in your world for a moment and look at it with attentiveness and won-der? Examine its torn edges and folds. Become aware of the way it reflects light and creates shadows within itself."

And finally, wonder becomes the gateway to creativity: "As you look carefully at the scrap of paper, is it possible to become fascinated with its qualities?"

Wonder is something we bring to the perception of the world, or perhaps the world gives this gift to us. It is a way of looking that can be applied to anything. If we find wonder in scraps of paper, spots on the floor, and pencil scribbles, we are ready to become fascinated with what already exists within our daily lives.

CREATIVE AMPLIFICATION OF THE WORKPLACE

Sometimes it is much easier to establish compassion for a scrap of paper than it is to seriously entertain a point of view that is contrary to ours. The workplace is an excellent frontier for art because the creative imagination typically has the most to offer in places where it is least recognized.

The best way to gain respect for the creative process at work is to concentrate on what the organization values and needs. One of the most important skills in the workplace involves the ability to understand the perspectives of others. The workplace can benefit from creative perception, which is capable of exploring subjects largely overlooked by the more conventional modes of organizational perception.

I am frequently asked, "What kind of art can a person make that is connected to work?" I suggest starting with art forms similar to what people already do in their lives that resonate with natural ways of expression.

When faced with a workplace where people may want to become involved in the practice of creativity but where environmental factors make it difficult for them to get "too far out there" in their expression, I recommend stories, simple role-playing exercises, and imagining the feelings and positions of others. Everybody has a story to tell that keeps us "anchored" in relatively safe and familiar experiences. It can be confusing for the average person to leap beyond an immediate setting and into free artistic expression without some direct link to experiences.

When we tell "stories" about an aspect of the workplace, our imagination is invited to contribute in a way that is not possible using the organization's formal communications. New realities, perceptions, feelings, and values are introduced. The view of reality and daily operations is widened through information that otherwise would not have a way of becoming part of the workplace. Storytelling flourishes in every institution, but it is rarely welcomed into the official organization with the exception of rituals celebrating the achievements of a person or group, memoirs, and other events that reinforce the organization's community life.

Many of the stories about the workplace are stock accounts that offer little new information. In contrast, creative stories enlarge the perception of experience as when employees tell more idiosyncratic and personal stories about their organizations: a day in the life of the water dispenser, the coffeemaker, the copy machine; how these articles view the surrounding community, what they see and hear; they have and information others do not have.

Imagination is increased when we look at the world from the perspective of something other than ourselves. However, most people have difficulty personifying inanimate objects. As they become more relaxed and confident in storytelling, they begin to think more poetically. In poetic expression it is natural to give a voice to objects and situations that are typically unappreciated.

Most of us begin to tell stories from our personal

perspectives, but as soon as we begin to openly explore the storytelling process, we realize there are untold stories behind the ones we normally tell, unknown even to ourselves.

Personal histories offer a comfortable opening to storytelling. What events brought you to this place and position? What was the environment like when you arrived? How has it changed? Has something been lost, improved? Involve other people and their perceptions of you and the environment. What has been comfortable for you and for other people at work? What has been difficult?

Explore your history in the organization by telling stories about other people. Others define us more than we realize. What we value and what we dislike in others can say more about who we are than attempting to describe ourselves. Include moments you found most enjoyable and most difficult. Tell the story of your most humorous experience at work, your most embarrassing moment, your greatest achievement.

Expand your history by telling it from the perspective of another person in the organization. This shift enables you to draw from the familiar basis of your experience, but the perspective of another person expands the scope of what is perceived and conveyed. We begin to realize that there are significant differences in how people perceive what appears to be the same event.

As a group leader, I make sure I demonstrate different ways of working and various possibilities for exploring a theme. I emphasize the importance of authentic communication and assure participants there is no right or wrong way to tell a story. Then I subtly introduce dramatic elements to the storytelling

process. The story naturally extends itself into body movements, role plays, and singing, which further its expression.

Visual art and poems may also emerge from storytelling or
from expressing a feeling about work. When I was frustrated
with the constant meetings I had to attend as an academic
dean, I painted a series of pictures expressing my feelings about
the situation. I exhibited them at the college, and they not only
helped me get through a difficult period, but also they gave
something back to others in the work community. I called the
series "art alchemies" and described how the creative process
transforms and makes good use of tension.

I encourage people to be aware of and use the space around
them when they are telling stories. I may start by sitting in a
chair, then get up to emphasize a point with my whole body,
and then sit again. Dramatic amplifications are most effective
when they emerge from a person's natural expressive style,
when they keep us grounded in who we are and where we are
at that moment.

When storytellers are describing situations involving
another person or what another person may feel, I encourage
them to adopt the other person's voice rather than try to
explain feelings. The shift into dramatic role playing seems to
be effortless and natural when it is used to more directly
express something that needs to be said. Storytellers generally
feel a sense of satisfaction when they portray a more accurate
expression of the feeling. The imagination of the event is also
heightened by the "presence" of the other person, achieved
through the dramatic device.

Exaggeration is a useful device in furthering the story's drama and emotion. Altering the tone of voice and the speed of speech as well as using expressive sounds brings the vocal element of artistic expression into the simple telling of a story. The same thing happens with body movement when we slow or speed the tempo, vary the degree of sensitivity or forcefulness in movement, etc. Exaggeration also introduces humor and its life-affirming medicine for the workplace.

Repeatedly, I discover that literal accounts of what did or did not happen are the most effective ways of blocking creativity. It is easy to fall into a judgmental and self-referenced worldview when we tell stories from the perspectives of our more habitual roles.

Fiction is another tool that can bring many benefits to exploring and understanding situations. Sometimes creative fiction, rather than literal description brings us much closer to the truth of a situation. Fiction may offer an anonymity that cannot be realized when we speak as ourselves. Imaginary figures can depict the facts and the real context of a situation better than our personal explanations, which tend to repeat stereotypic positions. It is easier to identify with a fictional character, a figure who may be a gathering point for qualities shared by many people.

I encourage people to define their workplaces by speaking from the perspectives of the people with whom they work. The strongest and most creative groups are the ones that most thoroughly acknowledge and articulate their differences. There are many practical benefits from establishing empathy with positions contrary to ours. In addition to feeling refreshed when we step out of fixed roles and expectations, we can use creative empathy to envision what can exist in the future.

When we watch films or read novels, we generally find it easy to empathize with the characters. But in our daily lives at work or even with our families, empathy is much harder to establish. The reluctance to let go of a point of view is no doubt caused by the fear of losing ourselves and becoming insignificant. Who am I if I do not have a point of view? The more insecure I am, the more I rigidly hold onto a fixed perspective and find it impossible to entertain the views of others.

A colleague describes herself as too empathetic. "I am always looking at everything from everyone else's point of view and I find it difficult to establish my own positions." I am not advocating a state of total relativism. The creative imagination requires a firm point of self-reference and the ability to perceive, interpret, and decisively integrate possibilities.

Creativity requires flexibility and a willingness to accept new ideas from outside our existing frames of reference. Another colleague once described how he tries to keep a soft hand on the tiller when he is involved in creative activities because the process will always lead him in unexpected directions. If a focus is too rigidly established, it becomes difficult to dislodge and change.

Ideally the practice of creativity brings an expansion and sharpening of perception, which improves the quality of a person's interactions with others and the environment. The creative practitioner strives to understand the perspectives of others, is always wary of the limitations of a narrow personal vision, and is constantly open to the refinements of perspective that take shape through exchanges with others. The practice of creativity teaches us that we do not act alone. Our creations and our lives are enhanced when we realize that everything in our environment is a source for imagination.

There is a mainstream of creativity moving through every day and every place. It awaits discovery and offers itself for transformation.

SHAUN MCNIFF, PH.D. is provost of Endicott College in Beverly, Massachusetts. An artist and internationally known figure in the creative arts therapies, he is the author of several books, including *Art as Medicine: Creating a Therapy of the Imagination* (Shambala, 1992), *Art-Based Research* (Jessica Kingsley, 1998) and *Trust the Process: An Artist's Guide to Letting Go* (Shambala, 1998).

Become a Creative Force

ROBERT FRITZ

We all have in us as part of our nature a deep desire to create, to bring something into being that never existed, to make something new. It may not be a painting, a novel, or a musical composition — the products typically associated with the creative process. We may want to create a new scientific explanation, a flower arrangement, a computer program, a business, or simply good health.

People are, by nature and instinct, creators. But very few people have been trained to create. Why has the creative process been made to seem like a mystery? Why have most people had such little exposure to it?

The process has been mystified in part because misconceptions have grown up around it. Many people think that great ideas descend from on high and visit special mortals who are blessed — or plagued — with sudden realization, vision, and inspiration. They fail to understand that creating is a process of which everyone is capable.

So how does one go about creating? The best way to learn to

create is by creating. Practice is always more important than theory. We can sit all day and talk about the creative process, but it is only when we start creating that we begin to have real knowledge, experience, and command of the subject. Only after involving ourselves in many experiences of creating can we become better at it.

There is no right way of painting, no right way of composing music, and no right way of creating your life. Much of what you will do will be based on personal style, preference, value, and desire. As you experiment with your path, you will become an expert in your creative process, and that is the only one that is truly relevant in your life.

At the same time, recognize that although the form of the creative process is not completely fixed, there are steps professional creators use most often.

KNOW WHERE YOU WANT TO GO

Professional creators start by knowing where they want to go. At the outset of creating, you must determine what you want to create and what end result you desire. Begin with a general idea, then envision some qualities and characteristics you want in the end result.

In this initial stage you are experimenting with ideas. You have not yet formed the end result you want. Instead, you are trying many end results to see how they play. The experience you gain by gradually forming your ideas helps you learn more about the end result you finally want to create.

IDENTIFY THE DESIRED END RESULT; ESTABLISH A VISION

From the many possibilities you might create, you settle on one, and only one. This is an evolutionary step in the creative process. After determining in a general sense what you want to create, you then establish a specific image about your end result. You may not have the details worked out fully, yet you need to know enough about the end result so you would recognize it if you saw it.

If you generally understand the end result you want, you can often live with several ideas over time until you determine which one will get you to your goal in the most satisfactory fashion. You will gain more and more focus over time. Some people think they must decide on an end result all at once and consequently settle on a first impression. First impressions are usually not well advised. Think a long time about your first impression before you turn it into a vision.

KNOW WHERE YOU ARE NOW

After you know what end result you want, you must assess what you currently have or where you are in relationship to the result you want. In the creative process as practiced by artists, inventors, composers, and architects, the current circumstances are always in view when the end result has been envisioned.

This assessment becomes an ongoing part of your creative process in that you should always be aware of the current state of the creation while it develops. In the beginning of the creative process there will be a discrepancy between what you want and what you have. This discrepancy forms a tension, a wonderful force because it naturally seeks resolution. As it does so, it generates energy that is useful in creating.

You will always have this structural tension in the beginning of the creative process, for there will always be a discrepancy between what you want and what you have. If you thoroughly understand your current reality (what you have), you can more easily organize your actions toward your final result (what you want). An essential part of the creative process is taking actions that will change reality. As the current reality changes, you, as creator, must be fluent with that change.

MOVE TOWARD YOUR CREATION

When you know what you currently have in relation to the end result you want, you are ready to take action. You may research useful approaches others have used, or you may experiment with an approach no one has taken.

Despite your desire to take action, however, your creative process may come to a screeching halt. Why? Inertia, fear of failure. Because there are no guarantees your actions will work, you may resist taking actions that will lead to your desired results. You may continue to plan and plan and plan.

You must forge ahead at this point, try out your ideas, and put your plans into action. Trying your ideas will help you invent ways to create the results you want faster, better, and more efficiently, moving you from theoretical speculation about what may work to real experience of what does and does not work. And creating is a continual process of learning what works and what doesn't.

LEARN FROM YOUR ACTIONS; BUILD MOMENTUM

After you have taken some sort of action, you can learn from that action. You are learning cognitively; you can observe the results of your actions and evaluate their effectiveness. You are also learning subconsciously. This kind of learning is essential because, as you become a creator, you begin to develop an instinct for the actions that work and the actions that don't. Creating is a skill that is cumulative. The more you create, the more you are able to create.

Each action you take is an experiment that leads to cognitive and subconscious learning. As your instincts increase, so does your ability to evaluate the merits of your actions. Evaluations lead to further adjustments, new or more actions, more learning, new evaluations, and so on, until you create the results you want.

The cumulative power of your actions helps build momentum. With momentum, you add energy and force to the next result you want to create. Without momentum you start over with each new creation. Many people begin again each time they set out to accomplish a new result because they have not learned how to create momentum during the creative process. One way to build momentum is to create a pattern of success by deliberately structuring a series of small successes on the way to your final goal. Each success adds to momentum, is easily assimilated, and helps build credibility and mastery.

Experienced creators know how to use their personal rhythms so they always have the energy needed to accomplish a project; novices go through a period of trial and error, mistakes, and blind alleys. But these situations provide needed learning. With time and experience, novices develop instincts for finding and taking the most effective actions.

KEEP MOVING

If you lose your way while you are creating, you can find your path again by establishing a place to go. This practice can produce tremendous movement, even if the place you have decided upon ends up being in the wrong direction. Not only can going in the wrong direction lead to a learning process, but through it you can gain more energy than if you did nothing until the "right" direction manifests itself. When you have a place to go, you create a dynamic that focuses energy and direction.

In the overview of the creative process this principle manifests itself in the difference between where you are and where you want to be. There is something in the human spirit that desires change and challenge. The human inclination toward change and challenge is best expressed in the creative process, because creating is a dynamic that helps to satisfy our spirit's desire to explore, to reach for new heights and depths of expression, and to become involved with life. When you become experienced in creating, you will discover that there are always new places to go — ones you had never imagined. Each new creation leads to possibilities of new places to go. The creative process opens doors; it never dries up or runs out of steam. The more places you go, the more places there are to go.

RECOGNIZE COMPLETION

Near the end of the creative process the rhythm you have generated often speeds up just before it slows and stops. Final decisions must be made. Then, if the creative process has been successful, it comes to an end. The completion stage calls for declaration. You as the creator of, and authority on, your vision can declare that the creation is complete. If you have been accurately measuring current reality against your vision, you can formally recognize that the creation matches your vision of the creation.

After the completion of your creation you develop a different relationship with it. You become the audience for your creation. You may or may not like what you have created. You may experience degrees of satisfaction that range from extreme disappointment to wild enthusiasm. Only living with the creation over time will tell the real story.

LOOK TOWARD THE FUTURE

Whether or not you are satisfied with your initial efforts, you can be assured of one thing: Having started to create, you'll want to continue. Creating is generative. The more people create, the more they want to create. The creative process generates momentum, energy, and thrust.

The creative process of more and more people is an incredible force. Creating opens new doors to new universes. When you are a creator, your relationship to life becomes more involved, more vital, more precious, more exciting, and more beautiful.

When you are a creator, there is never a time when life

becomes routine. There is always something new to learn, something new to create, and something new to love. So tap into your desire to create, look at things in different ways, experiment with the process, involve others, and experience the pleasure it will bring. By seizing the opportunities to create you'll find you're living life to the fullest — because creating is where the human spirit shines its brightest light.

✳

ROBERT FRITZ, composer and filmmaker, developed the Technologies for Creating® curriculum and wrote *Creating: A Guide to the Creative Process* (Fawcett, 1993) *The Path of Least Resistance* (Fawcett Books, 1989), *Corporate Tides* (Berrett Koehler, 1996), and *The Path of Least Resistance for Managers* (1999). He is the founder of the field of macrostructural patterns and structural consulting. His work has been used by Fortune 500 companies and nonprofit organizations, in Third World development, and in the lives of tens of thousands of people throughout the world.

Listening:
The Key to Deep Creativity

DON CAMPBELL

Listening is our bridge from the outer world to the inner world. Listening is a form of seeing, hearing, and feeling. We listen through our skin, our eyes, our noses, as well as our ears. Although ears are designed for balancing and hearing the world around us, it is the balancing and focusing of all the senses together that allow us to receive codes and patterns that are transformed into awareness, memory, and knowledge.

Music creates multiple levels of listening. A single piece of music can bring movement to the body, emotions to the heart, and memories to our consciousness. Learning to listen to music in creative ways provides the means for health improvement in the body, enhanced communication, and expression.

The origins of music predate language. The rhythms of walking, the pulses of our hearts, the utterances of pain, joy, and delight — all these natural patterns coupled with the natural sounds around us create the language of expression. Intuitively, we understand the language of sound, whether it is a distressed or joyous tone.

The ability to move from the outer world's sonic panoply into our inner feelings and language is an essential key in discovering the soul, the essence of creativity. Creativity in sound lies on the edge of awareness. The ability to trigger our thoughts from the sounds in our heads, as well as the ability to improvise on the ways we respond to the world, affects us in our spiritual, emotional, and physical lives. The soul of sound lies in its tone, the elongated hum that is never ending. It is a vibrational wave that supports the energy that organizes the universe. By making an elongated sound, an "o" or an "oooo" sound for five or six minutes, we can tap into that sense of vast energy from which all movement, melody, and rhythm originate.

Dr. Alfred Tomatis is the pioneer in the medical and acoustical study of listening. He found that, when one cannot focalize and organize auditory information emotionally and physically, one is out of balance mentally. He defines the function of the ear far beyond the normal tenets of hearing. He says it transmits energy, a cortical charge to the brain that keeps us consciously aware and stimulated. It integrates information from sound and motor movements to enable the development of verticality, laterality, and language. It establishes balance and equilibrium throughout the body. It is a discriminating organ that allows us to hear what we want to hear and often block out what we do not. Also, it allows us to locate ourselves spatially.

Hearing is vastly different from listening. Hearing is a passive sensation; listening allows us to perceive, focus, and name auditory information. As we move from hearing toward listening, our awareness is stimulated and we begin to focus on specific information. Memories and the ability to concentrate and respond to the world linguistically as well as musically depends on the ability to listen. This ability begins four and one-half months after conception, when the fetus is aware of rhythms, pulses, and sounds as well as higher frequencies of the mother's voice and some outer world sounds. Studies show that this in utero paradise can provide stimulation through music and sound that improves speech, coordination, and concentration after birth.

To listen creatively, experiment with your posture, your diet, and your moods. When you lie down, close your eyes, and listen, music takes on quite a different power. Images, memories, or new ideas may come to your mind. Listen to the same piece of music as you walk in nature and notice what the rhythm of your movements evokes. The same music can actively change the manner in which you think as well as move.

The soul of our creative impulses returns to these primary states of development. Rhythmic beats and movement, as well as lullabies, hymns, and play songs during our first years, are the most efficient connectors to our memory of an awareness that takes us into soul. Soul music is often caught in the pains of blues, the joy of Dixieland, and the sophistication of improvisations.

The tool that constantly evokes my creative impulse has been improvisation with sound. Taking patterns, rhythms, or melodies that we know well and give us comfort and letting them develop naturally into variations, into new territories of expression, creates pathways from our conscious knowledge into the unconscious source of vast potential. For instance, listen to

Mozart's twelve piano variations on "Twinkle, Twinkle, Little Star," originally a folk song, *"Ah, Vous Dirai-Je Maman"* (K. 265). This familiar little tune was a popular folk song at the time of Mozart's birth. You may have learned your ABCs through this simple melody. Now pick a task — writing, communicating, or a boring household task. Imagine yourself performing this task as you listen to "Twinkle, Twinkle." Then, close your eyes and listen to Mozart's variations. Let your mind wander, but constantly keep your task in your mind as you listen to the way in which Mozart embellished and creatively changed the rhythm and harmony of his theme. As you imagine doing this task, notice how the task changes as you listen to the music. For more complex insight, replay the variations as you move your body to the music. After each variation write key words or insights. You may want to mime the action of a skill you wish to improve. As simple as such an exercise is, it shows us that through imagery and movement we can tap the depths of our creativity with sound.

Music has all the universal components of language, emotion, and expression. There is music in silence. Our heartbeats and breath are an internal rhythm band. In the last seventy-five years, the world has become noisy from machines, radios, televisions, and endless stimulation. To withdraw in a natural silence for a few minutes before listening to music can greatly enhance your experience. Where the simple pulsations and natural sounds live without interruption, creates a safe space for us to explore the creative impulse, often called the Music of the Spheres.

The natural powers of listening are available through a variety of mind-body techniques. Meditation and hours of silence heighten awareness of our body rhythms and sounds. If our lives have been overstimulated, it may be very difficult to begin this form if inner listening. Silence and stillness can make many people nervous. Stimulating music, dance, or physical activity for twenty minutes before meditation often bridges the "nervous" gap.

The voice is a simple and powerful tool for calming the mind and invoking deep listening. Sit comfortably with closed eyes, exhale, and create a soft humming sound with a relaxed jaw. Allow a simple, quiet sound to begin, and imagine that you are exhaling tension. After two or three minutes, change to an "ou" sound. Continue for another three minutes. Then, just listen. Notice your breath, your mind, your body. You have modified your brainwaves into balance, calmed your body, deepened your breath. You are now prepared for listening better to your internal source.

SUGGESTED MUSIC:

PAULINE OLIVERAS, *Deep Listening* (New Albion).
DON CAMPBELL, *Essence* (Spring Hill Music).
———— *Music for the Mozart Effect Vol. III, Unlocking Creativity* (Spring Hill Music).

SUGGESTED READING:

DON CAMPBELL, *The Mozart Effect: Tapping the Power of Music to Heal the Body, Strengthen the Mind, and Unlock the Creative Spirit* (Avon Books, 1997).

PAULINE OLIVERAS, *Software for People* (Smith Publications, 1984).
ALFRED TOMATIS, *The Conscious Ear* (Station Hill Press, 1992).
PAUL MADAULE, *When Listening Comes Alive* (Moulin Press, 1993).

DON CAMPBELL is author of eight books. A classical musician, he has explored the powers of music in many cultures to see how the arts can be used more effectively to improve health and well-being throughout our lives. For more information on listening, contact the Mozart Effect Resource Center, 3526 Washington Avenue, St. Louis, MO 63103. Tel: (800) 721-2177.

Hearing the Audience

ROBERT GRUDIN

Literary history is a testament to dialog between writer and audience. From early times to the fifteenth century, manuscripts were often presented orally and literature was heard as much as it was seen. Cicero, the lion of ancient discourse, published exclusively in the language of friendship and forum: oratory, letter, and dialog. His penchant for personal revelation and reciprocal discourse would, centuries later, become thematic in Italian humanism. Renaissance humanists published orations, dialogs, and letters ad infinitum; Petrarch, their champion, wrote letters not only to friends but to the past and the future.

The sense of literature as a reciprocal transaction suffused itself into longer works. Machiavelli's mighty *Prince* was an extended handwritten letter, described as a "gift" and probably presented to its recipient (Lorenzo of Florence) in person. Boccaccio's *Decameron* advertises his physical charms and ends with the indecent proposal that his female readers should, if pleased by the text, "remember" him.

The notion of publication as dialog has survived, if intermittently, through the age of printing and beyond. The Shakespearean title page of *King Lear* (First Quarto, 1608), with its reference to an actual performance and its brief description of the popular character Edgar, is an early instance of advertising grounded on audience response. Charles Dickens scrapped the original ending of *Great Expectations* on the basis of a reading by his friend Edward Bullwer-Lytton. Montague Rhodes James recounted his ghost stories to his wards at Eton before committing them to books. In our times similar practices, though with somewhat less entertaining results, are de rigueur at academic conferences, where scholars often present their ideas orally before submitting them to journals. And now, in the meta-print age, hypertext and the Internet have turned reader response into a parlor game by encouraging readers to participate in the generation of the text.

The economics of publishing represents a larger but less personal kind of dialog. Hordes of otherwise silent readers speak with their cash, and critics, no matter what their interpretive skills, cannot compete in eloquence with the bell of the cash register. Successful books create channels for floating more ventures of the same sort, and it is the rare writer — a Rousseau, a Goethe, or a Byron — who does not capitalize on early success by repeating elementary formulas with nominal variation. That these channels erode an author's integrity is evidenced by the example of prolific Louis L'Amour, whose writing career was only momentarily interrupted by his death (books continue to be published under his name by Louis L'Amour Enterprises). The bestselling writer Stephen King has acknowledged this erosion by creating (in his novel *Misery*) a fictional image of himself as bestselling writer and then condemning this avatar to symbolic torments.

But another aspect of author-audience dialog is more interesting to me than any of the above. It is what one might call the wisdom of audience: the influence of audience on a writer's developing self-awareness. Direct and earnest audience response can renew writers' energy and commitment; it can also draw them out of the alienation many have come to associate with their craft. Audience response can give the writer a lesson in humanity.

I cannot describe this teaching clearly without reference to an archetypal literary experience that will seem mildly funny to anybody who has not been through it. Let us say that you are a professional writer with three or four respectable books in print. On a regional tour for your latest title, you have just given a talk to a bookstore audience of about thirty people, and now about fifteen are waiting in line as you sit at a desk, signing books.

You glance up at the line of people and exchange gazes with one reader who is clearly lit from within. (I say "reader" because gender, age, ethnicity, and social stratum are wholly irrelevant here, obliterated by a generic revelation.) The reader slowly approaches, eyes luminously fixed on you, looking at you as though you had been freshly minted in Paradise, looking the Look that says Thank you for having been born. You have never seen this reader before, but the Look knows you intimately, grasps what is special about you, perceives you not as an indifferent array of flesh and hair but as a breeding poetic soul.

At last you shake hands and the reader speaks. The discourse, made concise by time pressure, may reflect on any aspect of your work or the reader's experience, but the inner message is always, "You are part of my life."

The reader turns and departs. It's unlikely that you two will meet again. But a loop has been closed and things seem different from what they had been just moments before.

How do such encounters affect the writer? Ego-reinforcement would be an inaccurate answer. True, the ego flourishes on praise of all sorts, but arguably the meeting with reader takes a writer beyond ego. To understand why, we must examine typical literary egos or models of authorial identity. Of these, two are most familiar: the romantic model derived from the idea of artist as lonely hero, and the marketplace model derived from commerce and the performing arts.

In the romantic model, writers see themselves as brooding, solitary figures, married to art and in search of truth. Their encounters with audience, though sometimes seasoned with revelry or adulation, are ultimately oil-and-water affairs with no lasting effects. Why oil and water? Because the romantic model stipulates that writers have self-consciousness and social awareness, while audiences necessarily don't. Although such writers may feel grateful to their readers, it is subdued affection, arched across the channel of their alienation.

In the marketplace model, writers are technician-entrepreneurs whose goals are profit and fame. Like other performers and hucksters, they have an ambivalent view of audience: they need customers, but realize that successful selling involves a degree of concealment and deceit. They are willing to indulge and flatter their audiences, to flirt with them and clown it up in front of them, in quest of personal glory and financial triumph. But these activities make it impossible for writers to identify with their readership. If romantic writers are alienated by virtue of their self-conceit and self-consciousness, marketplace writers are alienated by virtue of their greed and ambition.

These models, both fueled by time-honored American fallacies and prejudices concerning privacy and profit, typically compete with each other in writers' minds, thereby giving the impression that they are not only opposite of each other but also comprise the only available viewpoints.

Audience encounters of the kinds described teach otherwise. The reader who approaches you lit from within has accepted something you offered and has been changed by it, gaining perhaps the ability to share it in new forms with others. Such writer-reader encounters, especially when repeated over several years, suggest a dialogic if not communitarian model of writing. In this model authors and books not only are discrete entities but also are participants in an evolving social reciprocity.

From the communitarian perspective, both the romantic model and the marketplace model shrink to rather puny ego-driven affairs; ego barriers dissolve into a continuum in which writing and reading are coequal in a pattern of mutual response. And this realization can carry psychological benefits. Phobic syndromes like writer's block and stage fright subside as performance is silently transmuted into contribution. The image of artist versus society gives way to a dialog reminiscent of earlier times.

This isn't to deny that reading and writing are solitary occupations. The emotional meeting between writer and reader is impossible until the reader has experienced a lonely revelation from a printed page, and this revelation cannot be brought about until the writer has spent long and exhausting hours of secluded composition. Yet all this solitude blossoms into a performance that is intensely and often intimately social. It is the paradoxical character of writing, at once intensely personal and inescapably social, that gives the profession its ambiguity and its appeal.

✳

ROBERT GRUDIN is a professor of English at the University of Oregon. His book, *The Grace of Great Things* (Houghton Mifflin, 1997), is part of an ongoing inquiry into creativity and human liberty begun in *Time and the Art of Living* (Houghton Mifflin, 1988) and continued in *On Dialogue: An Essay in Free Thought* (Houghton Mifflin, 1996). Grudin has written articles and essays for numerous magazines and newspapers including the *New York Times*.

Chapter  3

The Heart of Creativity

Every day we slaughter our finest impulses. That is why we get a heartache when we read those lines written by the hand of a master and recognize them as our own, as the tender shoots which we stifled because we lacked the faith to believe in our own powers, our own criterion of truth and beauty. Every man, when he gets quiet, when he becomes desperately honest with himself, is capable of uttering profound truths.

— Henry Miller

The Power of Failure

ERIC MAISEL, PH.D.

*C*reators are ambitious. They want to build great new worlds and make this old, flawed world a better place for their children. Truth, beauty, and goodness are their watchwords as are magic, passion, logic, intuition, knowledge, and humanity. Out of these building blocks they attempt to forge their spirited creative works, their songs and stories, their scientific theories and ten-foot sculptures. But the creator's painful secret, which may be God's secret as well, is that failure comes more often than success does. It is not easy to build new worlds. It is the opposite of easy.

Take writers. Writers with real accomplishments to their credit will be happy to tell us about all the books that didn't work, which may amount to half or two-thirds of their efforts. There were the books that were entirely written but that turned out to be seriously flawed because the writer wasn't ready or because the flaw just naturally appeared, as a flaw in pottery can appear after the firing process. Writers could tell us all about this, but we hate to hear these stories because it depresses and frightens us that so much failure is both possible and actually happens.

But there is no creativity without failure. Failure may even be at the heart of creativity, just as misfits and mutants have their honored places in the process of evolution. For creators, honoring the process means stumbling but getting up again, writing miserable books and painting miserable paintings, throwing out ideas and beautiful lines that do not fit, nursing depression and surviving depression, living through good manias and bad manias, having their work insulted (Today I received an edited manuscript whose margins were peppered with "lame!"s and "flabby!"s), and a thousand other things that are inevitable parts of the process. It means accepting all of this and influencing for the better that which can be influenced.

Dishonoring the process means wanting it all to be otherwise and acting as if it could be otherwise. It means not showing your work when it is ready because of fear of its reception. It means researching instead of thinking or making things up instead of researching. It means being a drunk six days out of seven. It means not being arrogant enough to create and being too arrogant to listen to others. It means not doing what one knows one should do and doing what one knows one shouldn't. Above all, it means refusing to accept failure in the creative process and the creative life. Mere mortals may want to avoid failure, but gods and creators accept that failure is their lot more times than they can count.

Creators can accept this intellectually. But their actual failures hurt. After a well-received concert of Handel's music, the king exclaimed to the famous composer, "The audience was very greatly entertained!" A downcast Handel replied, "Did I only entertain them? I had hoped to make them better!" What sort of odd reaction is that? It is the reaction of a creator with the loftiest ideals feeling as if he'd failed, even though the audience was shouting its approval. When even successes can feel like failures, what a strain is put on creators!

I believe that letting the secret out of the bag and actively thinking about all of this — the nature of the creative process, the naturalness of failure, the way that part successes often do not feel good enough — helps us to survive. But it is hard to think about. I remember chatting in an airport restaurant with the publisher of several of my books about a book I was considering writing. I had done a pair of books called *Fearless Creating* and *Fearless Presenting* and was thinking about a third in the "series" to be called *Fearless Thinking*. We concluded that such a book would be too hard to sell. Too few people would be willing to suffer the uncomfortable feelings that come with trying to think.

But if we do not think about the place of failure in the creative process, then when we write a miserable first novel or draw people who look like ducks (when we wanted them to look like people) we'll chastise ourselves, retreat from future efforts, and shut off our creativity. If we do not understand that failure, mistakes, missteps, wrong turns, bad ideas, shoddy workmanship, half-baked theories, and other sad events are part of the process, if we romanticize the process and make believe that creativity comes with a happy face, then when we encounter our own rotten work we will be forced to conclude that we do not have what it takes. But we have what it takes. What it takes is learning and recovering from our mistakes.

I teach a class each semester called "Personal and Professional Assessment." It is a class for middle-aged adults who are returning to school to get their bachelor's degrees after a long absence from the classroom. Their primary task in my class is to write five experiential learning essays on five subjects of their choosing. These managers, policewomen, firefighters, wine makers, and salespeople have written very little for years and strongly doubt they have the skills to do the required writing. I start right in and teach them essay basics — how to analyze, synthesize, and evaluate, how logical arguments are built — but I also let them know that their first efforts may look wretched. I ask them to succeed, but I give them real permission to fail.

I encourage them to think about the subjects they've chosen to write about — to grow quiet and to begin writing — and to ignore the horribleness of their first drafts. Slowly but surely they manage to do this. They begin to think about a subject like divorce or child abuse in a deep way and to stop thinking about the skills they lack. They begin to quiet their inner demons. They start to feel less frightened as their computers boot up and less intimidated by the blank screens when they appear. They continue to feel a little anxious, but they learn that such anxiety is normal. Maybe it isn't even anxiety. Maybe it's just excitement! Whatever those butterflies mean, they really don't matter.

These engaged student writers go deeply and write well.

They focus on the subjects at hand and not on themselves or their frailties. They start to say things like "All right, I've bitten off a big thing here. But no problem!" Rather than doubt themselves, they focus on their ideas. Despite these improvements, they still sometimes write not-very-good essays. But often they write well. Some of their essays are as good as the pieces you see in journals and magazines. This accomplishment is remarkable and is a sign that almost anyone can do the writing he or she dreams of doing, if only the inevitable failures that arise can be normalized, embraced, and forgiven.

Books do not go unwritten because the writer has trouble remembering whether to use *its* or *it's*. They do not go unwritten because the writer has trouble deciding whether, in the world she is creating, she will have her rose bushes flower in winter or lie dormant. They do not go unwritten because the writer can't write sentences (we all can), because the writer can't write paragraphs (we all can), or because the writer can't write chapters (we all can, with practice). Books go unwritten because the writer is afraid of failing. He is afraid of disappointing himself, wasting his time, and looking like an idiot. The specter of failure kills his chance for success.

We agree with Handel: creators have profound work to do. We set our sights high. We want to express the mystery of reality in such a way that human beings become better. We want to make worlds, to explain this world, to catch magic as it flies past, and to become living magic. We are not conceited in holding these views; we are simply identifying and affirming our role in the culture. What is that role? To guard the good and to make things better. But to create and to become a role model we need to think about failure more than we do. We need to think about its reality, its naturalness, even its ubiquity. Failure is a painful subject, but to keep secret about it is worse.

If each success requires ten failures, then count each failure as a blessing on the road to success. For our successes to mount, so must our failures.

✳

DR. ERIC MAISEL is a creativity consultant and the author of *Fearless Creating* (Tarcher/Putnam, 1995), *Fearless Presenting* (Backstage Books, 1997), *Affirmations for Artists* (Tarcher/Putnam, 1996), and *A Life in the Arts* (Tarcher/Putnam, 1994). His forthcoming books include *Deep Writing* (Tarcher/Putnam, Spring 1999) and *Living the Writer's Life* (Watson-Guptill, Fall 1999).

Dr. Maisel can be contacted by fax or phone at (925) 689-0210, by E-mail at amaisel@sirius.com, or by mail at P. O. Box 613, Concord, CA 94522-0613.

Taming the Lion

JEAN LIEDLOFF

*I*ronically, I have probably learned more about the creative process from wrestling with writer's block than any other way. Several clients, too, have consulted me about blocks while trying to write a Ph.D. thesis or other pieces. This has started me pondering the anatomy of the creative block and of creativity itself. I have come to see that the mysterious biological process by which inspired work is produced can be used more effectively when the process is better understood.

A block is what we call the frustrating time when the conscious mind, or will, does not succeed in getting the unconscious mind, the creative part, to produce the work. I shall talk here about writers, but the principles that apply to blocking and unblocking creativity hold true as well for painters, composers, scientists, inventors, and poets, and whenever someone attempts to create, not just transmit or copy, a work. The product must be manifested out of a source in oneself.

Suppose you accepted an assignment to write a magazine article. If you understand the exigencies of your creative process, you know it requires about a week to produce the 2,000 words you will want in the article. You will make the assignment as clear as possible to the "beast" (as I call my creative source), defining the range of content to be included and you may look through copies of the magazine to remind yourself of the magazine's house style and the general character of the readership. You may need to conduct research. All these matters, which I call clarifying the assignment, should be done before you attempt to write.

Think of the conscious mind as the lion tamer, the creative department of the unconscious mind, the lion. The desired product is the circus act: the lion jumping through hoops or sitting on command. The mind of the lion is very different from that of the tamer, so it is the task of the tamer to learn how the lion's mind works, at least enough to get it to obey and perform its tricks. Thus, the writer must learn from experience how the beast works, and what it requires to produce the desired words.

One requirement is having enough time. With experience you can pretty well guess how much time a project will need for preparation in the unconscious before you can summon it into consciousness and then to paper. But you cannot say to the beast "Sometime next week" or "You know what I mean." The beast is a different kind of mind, and it works best with a precise instruction like "I will write this next Tuesday at ten A.M." Then it is important to be there at ten A.M on the appointed day, not five minutes early or two minutes late, but respectfully keeping your agreement with the beast whose character it is to take things literally. The words are then ready and waiting.

I am thinking of one example among professional writers I have known, who did not know how to tame his beast . . . and two who did. Dwight MacDonald wrote mostly for the *New Yorker* or *Esquire*. For years he suffered the same consequences because he lacked mastery over the rules of the beast. He had, say, three months to hand his editor an article on a given subject of a given length. The subject and length requirements were suitable to feed to the beast, but the deadline was a precise date when it had to be finished. Dwight always meant to write when it was convenient and at a leisurely pace in the more than ample time allowed. But for decades of magazine writing, it seemed, he never was able to fulfill that intention. He always procrastinated despite the growing pressure of guilt that tainted whatever he was doing while he put off writing. His beast had been told only the deadline, so it produced the work in the last two days, exactly the time required to meet it. Dwight worked day and night for those last days to finish the piece, handed it in, and then collapsed, exhausted, promising Gloria, his wife, and himself never again to wait until the last minute. But he continued to repeat the faulty message to the beast. He was, in effect, saying "You know what I mean" to the lion at his creative source, instead of telling it exactly when to go to work. And the lion kept obediently meeting the deadline literally while Dwight and Gloria kept paying the price in stress, guilt, and exhaustion.

The two writers who made better deals with their respective beasts are Graham Greene, the acclaimed English writer, and Alberto Moravia, the well-known Italian. Graham Greene told me that he always wrote "exactly 750 words a day when I am writing. If I have written 751 one day, I write 749 the next." This is a perfect example of the respectful attitude the conscious mind must take toward the very different mentality of the creative unconscious if it is to be persuaded to do its stuff. Comprehending the dual character of the mind and permitting each function to play its part, for which it evolved produces a smooth, quite seamless performance.

Moravia, like many others who have learned to tame their lions, began to write every morning at nine A.M. and stopped at the stroke of one. He would then have lunch, go to the beach, meet friends, and enjoy the rest of the next twenty hours while his creative source prepared the words in time for his next day rendezvous with it at nine A.M.

Four hours a day, I have often heard, is pretty much the optimum one can expect from the beast without squeezing it too hard and causing a backlash (or tail-lash), resulting in diminished quality, blocks, or other signs of rebellion. But there are many exceptions, and one must humbly figure out what one's own beast demands before it will cooperate. I have heard, though not from him (or his lion's mouth), that Lawrence Durrell wrote *Justine* in six weeks, pressing on "day and night" until it was complete. Some writers' beasts insist upon producing only at night, others only in specific places — in town or in the country, indoors or in a gazebo at the bottom of a garden, facing a wall or beside a window. But whatever your beast demands, do not try to reason with it. The genius that resides in Homo sapiens is impervious to reason.

✳

JEAN LIEDLOFF is the author of the groundbreaking book *The Continuum Concept: In Search of Happiness Lost* (Perseus Press, 1986). She is head of the Liedloff Society for the Continuum Concept, a nonprofit organization for people who want to make the Continuum Concept part of their lives. She has a private practice on her houseboat in Sausalito to educate and serve the public — especially parents and parents to be — by advocating the principles of the Continuum Concept in childrearing. She can be reached at (415) 332-1570 or visit her website at www.continuum-concept.org.

Uncertainty — Building Creative Behavior

LINDA A. FIRESTONE, Ph.D.

*C*reativity is found where the search for a new and better ordering of life exists. That ordering, or more accurately, reordering, may be internal, it may be physical, or it may be aesthetic. For example, if a woman seeks to alter her emotional responses, she may have to change how she treats and uses her body. Perhaps she must stop talking about her desire to do something and instead sit down and produce a product with her hands: a floral arrangement, a new recipe, or a drawing. Perhaps she needs to study a discipline she has loved only from a distance. These reorderings are accompanied by feelings of uncertainty and fear, but in the end they are always a creative experience, one that offers her the opportunity to examine herself and her creativity intimately. In this context, creative behavior also takes shape when a new ordering of a woman's life occurs — when she has a baby, is divorced, loses a parent, moves to a new town, changes her career.

The strain and confusion may cause a woman to look at her life and wonder what the future holds. She may feel unsure of her strength and capacity to give shape to her future. Feeling vulnerable and at risk, she may view her actions as wrong or as ineffectual. It is precisely at these times, and by the manner in which she negotiates the uncertainty, that her path and the quality of her journey will be determined. The result of her transition through uncertainty contains the expression of her creative spirit.

Recently, I read about Barbara McClintock, a scientist who studied cell development and cell growth patterns. The strength of her vision and her ability to pursue her work were reflected in her willingness to pursue a course of research that was unconventional. She openly dedicated herself to seeking out the essence of living organisms that occurred in cells that were anomalies. These cells did not fit into the norm. Their growth patterns were illogical, unclear. She loved those cells, whose growth defied the conventional developmental patterns. Their unusual developmental manner challenged her on new levels. They taught her how to see with her eyes, her heart, and her head. Her dedication to seeking knowledge and understanding led her to be creative in her scientific approach. She was criti- cized for being highly unconventional; she used her intuition as a way of initiating her path through the undiscovered world of cell development. Because she was sensitive to the potential for becoming that is found in the place of uncertainty, she learned to use her creative essence in concert with her head. She unrav- eled the mystery of those different kinds of cells. Despite the derision shown to her for her work and her beliefs from more conventional scientists, she won a Nobel prize.

The derision aimed at her work and her approach was

based upon an unwillingness to see, to hear, and to think in a new way. It reflected a rigid response to the unknown. Not until years later when other scientists followed her path of seeing were they able to understand cell growth in all its complexity. Scientists who were unwilling to challenge themselves or the scientific rules because they were unwilling to creatively confront uncertainty were left out of a personal and scientific truth about the universe. The cells demonstrated a far more complex reality of the universe than could be comprehended and absorbed by taking the easiest, the most traditional method of observation and evaluation. The very essence and existence of those cells could be apprehended and seen only through creative seeking.

In pursuing the unknown, Barbara found her humanity, her strength, and her creative abilities. The questions for both Barbara and the world were housed in the realm of uncertainty. She did not interpret a lack of knowledge or understanding negatively. She found joy, excitement, satisfaction, and creative expression in moving toward uncertainty. She emerged from her journey a wiser, more complete, creative woman.

The example of Barbara's vision, her commitment to herself and to her creative expression, can be translated by other women into everyday terms. Think of it for a moment. Do you, at times of uncertainty, rise to the challenge before you? Do you assume the worst and retreat into familiar habits and thought patterns? Do you find yourself looking into the unknown and seeing the edge of the abyss? Is that image also accompanied by an assumption that you are doomed to fall if you go one step further? One the other hand, do you meet the challenge, despite your fear, with a belief that the path, though rugged, will lead you to a more fulfilling life?

Remember that times of uncertainty are invariably attended by feelings of fear and trepidation. But the truth existing within the unknown territory is one that contains movement outward to the world and forward in seeking possibilities. The time of uncertainty holds an expansive path. Movement outward and forward happens when a woman relies upon her creative spirit for direction and clarification to meet the challenge. Then she can alter her internal or external environment (or both) and use those times of uncertainty.

The self-knowledge, acknowledgment, and strength a woman gains from having moved through the moments of uncertainty are what makes these times powerful, creative experiences. Change comes only as part of a creative process. It is the reflection of a deep-seated need, one that demands attention and satisfaction. Unfortunately, most women are not taught or encouraged to draw upon their creative spirits as tools for negotiating uncertainty and change. They do not believe themselves capable of creative behavior, thereby limiting their potential. Sadly, most women have not learned to seek out and express their essential creative spirits. Because of the weight of societal or parental expectations, many women are set on a path of limited potential. They are not curious and adventurous. They do not actively seek their creative spirit and do not know how to express their essential creative nature. The positive potential contained within the difficult, uncomfortable times is left unacknowledged and abandoned.

Ironically, creative behavior exists because of uncertainty. It is the means to solving a problem, whether artistic, aesthetic, economic, political, physical, or emotional. Creative behavior orders chaos and structures change. Wishing to live a creative vibrant life, a woman must come to terms with the uncertainty inherent in creative behavior. She must take risks, be patient, be acknowledged, and act upon her need to express that which is unique about herself. She must be able to disregard what others may think about her desire and persevere through disappointment. These are qualities that make creative behavior possible. The determination and inner need to share one's self leads a woman into and out of the unknown, the space of uncertainty.

Instead of looking at the times of uncertainty, often characterized as chaotic, emotional, and even physically draining, a woman can gather her inner resources, celebrate herself, and confront the unknown with optimism. Studies have shown that people who live their lives participating in what they believe to be creative behavior are mentally, physically, emotionally, and spiritually healthier than those who repress and try to control. Creative behavior teaches a woman that she has within her the strength and wherewithal to move through times of uncertainty and emerge renewed with a new and cherished sense of her completeness. The mistake many women make when confronted with uncertainty is to seek control and order by relying upon old responses. Unaware of what she is doing, she turns to a path, a process, or a way of seeing and understanding her life that no longer fits. The result is that she tries to replicate the past even though it may no longer be satisfying or healthy for her.

Jenny Winter, a psychologist writing about creativity in research, offered her readers four lessons that encourage and reinforce creative thinking. I have adapted her concepts so they relate to living a creative life and meeting times of uncertainty and change with courage and enthusiasm:

1. Be willing to seek out a new path.
2. Be willing to take small and large risks, and challenge your understanding of your situation. Do not judge the results of taking a risk.
3. Focus on the path you have traveled. What physical, emotional, intellectual, and spiritual experiences have you had in the process?
4. Look closely at all events that have touched your life in the process and stay open to new understandings.

Barbara McClintock knew that the exceptions in cell development were exciting and enlightening. She knew that a deeper meaning for her life would be found by unlocking the growth pattern of those cells. The times of uncertainty that you may experience in your life hold clues to your growth as a creative woman. Embracing these times can rejuvenate, expand, and strengthen your creative spirit. The spaces of uncertainty that fill and alter your life are the building blocks that shape your path to expressing your creative potential. Appreciate and welcome them.

✴

LINDA A. FIRESTONE, PH.D. has a variety of published works solely related to women. She is a freelance writer, researcher, grant writer, and lecturer. She is a part time faculty member at Nova Southeastern University, as well as a member of the Board of DIrectors for the House of Hope/Stepping Stone (long term residential facilities for homeless, indigent, HIV/AIDS infected men and women suffering from alcohol and substance abuse). She is currently researching her next book the focus of which is women in recovery. Her latest work *Awakening Minerva: The Power of Creativity in Women's Lives,* (Warner, 1997) celebrates creativity in women.

The Creative Soul Lives in the Shadows

AVIVA GOLD, A.T.R-B.C.

Those of us called to create authentic art in Western culture have been up against formidable challenges. To express the uninhibited depths of our originality and soul, we must risk being unacceptable to a prevailing, polite status quo and thousands of years of rigid Judeo-Christian ethic. To do our job as artists well, we need to be outspoken, meticulously honest, and authentically emotional, which means that we and our art may express rage, grief, destruction, depression, death, and sexuality. We may need to paint African mask faces in midnight black and blood red. Our art may show up as flamboyant, aggressive, morbid, corny, disgusting, provocative, and totally outrageous.

These artistically necessary traits and topics are, in our culture, referred to as the shadow side of life and the shadow side of our personalities. These shadows have the connotation of being negative, unpopular, unnecessary, and threatening. We know that death and destruction are natural, essential, and life-fostering aspects of nature. We know that full expression of all aspects of ourselves brings physical, emotional, and spiritual health to our culture and ourselves. Yet, there is a history and association of alcoholism, suicide, and insanity with being a "real" artist. Might this be the result of, first, our commercial culture placing a chosen few real artists on pedestals and then viewing them with both awe and suspicion? Second, because we collectively deny the artists in ourselves, don't we think of culturally recognized artists as outsiders, unpredictable and possibly dangerous? We are uncomfortable with the very honesty we expect from them.

I know that the full expression and enthusiastic acceptance of these shadows is essential for the health and survival of art and humanity. For me the soul of creativity lives in the shadows and must be continuously mined, embraced, and expressed. I see those of us in our culture who take creative risks in art making as trailblazers, cultural symbolic steam valves, blood letters, permission givers, inspirational leaders, and visionaries. But we pay a high price. I believe the health, emotional stability, and prosperity of artists in our culture have suffered because of the subtle societal sanction and fear of this essential shadow material, which artists are naturally called upon from within to express.

There are indigenous peoples in whom the expression of what we call shadow is respected and embraced, and those who express it are respected and embraced. There is also no distinction between being human and being an artist — everyone is an art maker. Often these people are dark skinned, representing the shadow side of white establishment. We have a lot to learn from these people as we do from our shadows.

In addition to the important expression of culturally perceived shadows is the expression of our personal shadows — often harder to see. Our shadows could be any aspect that we do not recognize or value, such as being funny, loving, silly, cheerful, zany, wild, vulnerable. Some people can show these sides only when they are drunk or otherwise anesthetized. It is transformative when we can paint them.

Art is the embodiment of raw materials into a work of soul. A transformation occurs. The absolute necessity of embracing the shadow, of embracing what appears to be the hideous monster for transformation to occur is depicted throughout history in myth and fairy tale. The best known is "Beauty and the Beast." There is a Beauty and a Beast in each of us. The Beast started out as a helpless, misunderstood child, our honest, emotional, outspoken side that through repeated sanctions went underground. That naturally alive, creative, honest, sensuous child remained in our unconscious, under a spell, never dying but growing uglier to get our attention in nightmares and spontaneous flareups, addictions and symptoms. Then one day, maybe because of a crisis, we are face-to-face with the now ugly fearful monster. We are locked in a castle — or in front of a canvas — face-to-face.

The act of painting the Beast as it is — not making it pretty — is your liberation. Looking into the eyes and heart of your jailer beyond the mask will unlock the true gift hidden within. Your original creative soul has been hidden within the monster, and acknowledging and expressing this part of you allows you and your art to heal and transform so that the true prince (or princess) is born.

So, the more you make conscious and welcome with compassion the unconscious aspects of your self, the more free and versatile becomes your creative expression. The more you creatively express these hidden aspects, the more soul and authenticity enters your art. The less fear you have of revealing anything and the less energy you spend in inhabitation, the more energy is available for free expression. In the twelve-step program there is a wise expression: "You are only as sick as your secrets." I would say, "Your creative limitations are only as great as your unexpressed shadows."

The following is an example of how allowing myself to paint personally and culturally disturbing images — painting my dark angel — cured me of arthritis. Fifteen years ago I hit a very frightening period in my life. After years of being a single mom my children were leaving the nest. I had also just initiated a long-term separation from my dysfunctional parents after a lifetime of emotional abuse. I was experiencing poor health, which included low energy, digestive disturbances, and painful arthritic symptoms in my hands and other joints.

Although I had been practicing spontaneous painting for several years, the themes were all inspirational and uplifting: colorful and sensual aspects of the Goddess or Wild Woman archetype. But now in the midst of fear and despair, while painting I felt compelled to spill forth what was to be a most demonic scene. With my usual commitment not to censor what my brush wanted to depict, I found myself painting in pitch black a most tortured, tormented figure. It was eviscerated, with body cut open, guts spilling out, torture and tears on the face, and excrements of every disgusting description from each orifice. While painting I felt very emotional and nauseated. I felt compelled to add paper on all sides of the painting, making room for strange little men with pointed hats that were drinking the body fluids. I thought they were attacking and torturing me. When I completed the painting, I noted that in addition to being a visually powerful painting, its shape was a Celtic cross, which is also the shape of the Red Cross.

Although I was convinced of my insanity while painting, I was amazed to wake up the next morning with my arthritis gone (never to return) and a feeling of a positive shift in my life in general.

Many years later I showed a slide of that frightful painting at a conference at which a scholar in Native American mythology was present. After my presentation he told me that the creatures I had painted were identical to the little helpers the Plains Indians medicine people call in to remove toxins from the body while they perform healing. It all made perfect sense. What I thought were my torturers were really my saviors in disguise. Unfortunately, I needed to feel so desperate that I felt I had nothing to lose in order to paint my dark angels, an aspect of my shadow.

I believe that physical symptoms, dreams, and creative imagery all come from the same source: They are all expressions of the soul. Alter one and you alter all. That is why, when painting as a healing ritual in which you risk expressing your shadows, true healing occurs. What you think is your slayer is your redeemer. Liberate your shadows and you liberate your creative soul. Liberate your creative soul and you liberate the world.

I think our global survival depends on the acceptance and encouragement of safe and sacred expressions of shadow. Can you imagine a world in which the leaders in business, politics, religion, and science routinely painted, danced, and sang their hearts out? Hearts would be burst open. It would be hard to have wars, mistrust and deceit. The creative soul would then live in light and dark and all the colors in between.

✳

Artist-therapist AVIVA GOLD, MFA, CSW, A.T.R.-B.C., is the author of *Painting from the Source: Awakening the Artist's Soul in Everyone* (HarperCollins, 1998). Her lecture and worldwide workshop schedule takes her to personal growth centers such as Omega Institute, Open Center, Kripalu, and Common Boundary. She has also helped at workshop intensives in Greece and Belize, and her quarterly newsletter is mailed to 2,700 subscribers. Articles about Gold and *Painting from the Source* have appeared in numerous publications including *New Woman, Art Times,* and *New Age Journal.*

Chapter  4

The Healing Force
of Creativity

*Art provides a healing force which aids both the
maker and the viewer.*

— Richard Newman

The Healing Power
of Creativity

ECHO BODINE

C reativity is one of the most valuable tools we have to aid us in our healing process, and yet many of us never consider using it to heal our pain.

Creativity can be simple, playful, colorful, out of the lines or in the lines kind of fun, or it can be serious: designing a building, creating a community, developing a strategy, or writing a screenplay. It's taking a piece of wood and building furniture, a birdhouse, or a fence; constructing a piece of cloth into curtains, a dress, or a Halloween costume; taking a blank piece of paper and painting a picture, writing a poem, or composing music. It's dressing a mannequin, planting a garden, landscaping a yard, decorating a room, making a scrapbook, baking, designing a blueprint, sculpting, cooking, quilting, dancing, inventing, advertising, getting dressed, budgeting money, building boats, brainstorming, carpentry, stitchwork, putting up decorations for the holidays, making mud pies, framing a picture. There are so many ways to express our gift of creativity; unfortunately, there are so many people who never think of themselves as creative beings!

When I was in high school, art class was one of my worst subjects. I'm one of those people who has to see something before she can visualize it, so coming up with original projects was always tough for me. In my senior year, I got an F on my class project along with a note that said I had no imagination and that I should pursue other interests besides art. Unfortunately, I took that to mean I had no creative ability and believed it for years. Anytime I thought about taking a creative class like cake decorating or creative writing, I always felt that it would be a waste of time, so I wouldn't even try.

When I was twenty-five years old and in my first year of recovery from alcoholism, my sponsor suggested I get some kind of hobby kit. I told him that I didn't have any creative ability, and he said he didn't care about that, he was more concerned about my lack of patience and thought that learning how to follow instructions would be a good start. I couldn't see how this was going to keep me sober, but I bought a candle-making kit anyway. I wasn't very good at slowing down long enough to read the directions, and in my impatience I kept thinking there were a lot more important things to do in life than learn to make candles, so I convinced myself that it was a waste of time and put the kit in the closet. The next time I saw my sponsor he asked me how my new hobby was coming and I told him I was not only not creative, but I also didn't have time for trivial things like hobbies. He told me my lack of patience was going to hinder me for the rest of my life and to go back and give it another try.

As it turned out, making myself slow down and read each step of the instructions was one of the best things that ever happened to me because I saw the value of slowing down to do something creative, and I realized over the course of weeks and months that followed that I was very creative. Each candle I made opened and stretched my imagination a little more. Colors, scents, working with the wax — it always felt so good to come up with new ideas and see how they would turn out. The more creative I became the more patient I seemed to be. I was also developing a confidence in myself I hadn't had. Discovering that I was creative and learning the value of patience was opening a whole new world for me.

The healing power of creativity helped another part of my life: the depression I had suffered from most of my life. I found that getting totally lost in a creative project or making something for someone else always seemed to ease the feelings of hopelessness and despair, even if it was only temporary. Working on a creative project gave me something to look forward to and a goal to strive for.

The other area of my life that was steadily improving as I whittled away at my candles was my spirituality. My conversations with God became longer and longer, and I would also sit in the silence for long periods, listening to the still small voice within for guidance. Sitting, creatively working on a project became prayer and meditation time for me, and I loved it.

Looking back throughout my adult life, I see how much of my healing process has involved creativity in one form or another. Journal writing is a wonderful creative tool for helping to heal old emotional scars. Writing or drawing pictures of old memories can be a marvelous way of healing and releasing them.

Letting the inner child express its memories through drawing, cutting out pictures from magazines, painting, or coloring can be excellent ways to help express all that is trapped inside.

When we give ourselves permission to go into our healing process, creativity can help ease the pain. It's like putting a soft edge on an otherwise painful one. In my second book, *Passion to Heal*, I have an exercise at the end of each chapter designed specifically to help readers express their pain through creativity. Instead of storing those old hurts and pains in our bodies, it is so important to get them out. Yes, we have therapists who help us do a lot of releasing, but when it's 1:00 A.M. and we can't sleep, it's very empowering to know there is something we can do on our own to help ease and heal pain, and that is to get out of bed and get creative with the pain. Write it out, draw it out, color it out, paint it out. Whichever creative way you choose to get it out will help tremendously.

A few years ago, I went through a painful breakup of a relationship. I did not want to stay stuck in the pain. I wanted to move past it as quickly as possible. I prayed for guidance as to what would be most effective, and I was directed to make a scrapbook of the relationship. I gathered all the pictures I had taken during our time together, memorabilia, jewelry he'd given me, anything I could find around the house that reminded me of the relationship. Instead of avoiding the restaurants or other places we had frequented, I went to all of them and got some kind of little memento, like a napkin, matches, or stationery. I bought lots of stickers, some with words, others just expressive thoughts or shapes.

Every night I would shut off the phones and TV and would creatively write about the entire relationship, as if I were writing a story. "Once upon a time" was how I started the scrapbook, and I wrote about the entire relationship from beginning to end, pasting photographs, drawing pictures, inserting symbolic stickers wherever appropriate. I wrote about each significant place we went to, writing story after story, taping everything momentous, including the jewelry, into the scrapbook. Sometimes I laughed as I wrote my memories; other times I cried. After doing that five nights in a row, two or three hours per night, I felt free. I had gone through every stage of our relationship and was able to be very honest with myself about it. I not only healed much quicker than any other breakup I had gone through, but also I learned a lot about myself.

There were times since writing that scrapbook that I have found myself romanticizing about the relationship. It was always helpful to go dig it out of the attic and reread it. That creative process helped me stay in touch with the reality of how it *really* was.

We were created from the Creator of all the universe, so it stands to reason that creativity is as much a part of us as are our bodies, minds, and souls. We all have within us the same creative genius that God has because we come from God. It's truly amazing when you stop and think about all the possibilities this gives us. Using our imagination and expressing our creativity can alleviate stress, improve our health, and bring joy to our relationships. Creativity can be comforting, nurturing, happy, and fun. People don't stay sad for too long when they're creating because creativity is a happy energy.

The next time you're around a sick child, give him or her coloring books, some crayons, and stickers, and watch them get lost in a world of creativity. Slowly they forget how bad they feel because their minds are swirling with colors, shapes, and new possibilities.

The next time you're not feeling so well, whether it's mentally, emotionally, physically, or spiritually, try doing something creative yourself. There is a certain magic to the healing power of creativity, and it doesn't cost any more than the price of a tablet and some crayons! God bless you on your healing journey.

✳

ECHO BODINE is a spiritual healer, psychic, teacher, author, and ghostbuster. She has written three books: *Hands That Heal*, which teaches others how to channel healing energy; *Passion to Heal: The Ultimate Guide to Your Healing Journey* (New World Library, 1993) and *Echoes of the Soul: The Soul's Perspective of Life, Death, and Life After Death* (New World Library 1999). She also writes a monthly column, "Ask Echo," for *Twin Cities Wellness* newspaper and *WholeLife News* in England. The main focus of her work today is lecturing and teaching workshops. Because of her work as a ghostbuster, she has appeared on several national TV shows such as *Sally Jesse Raphael, Sightings, Encounters, The Unexplained,* and *NBC's The Other Side.*

Creativity —
The Healing Journey Inward

JAN PHILLIPS

*I*t's not easy these days, making time for creative work. Voices call us from everywhere demanding our attention, energy, hours. And many of us, somewhere along the path, got the message that making art was self-indulgent, so we relegate our creative projects to the bottom of the list. It becomes the thing we get to when the laundry is done, the books are in order, the groceries bought and put away.

We get so caught up in the flurry of our lives that we forget the essential thing about art — that the act of creating is a healing gesture, as sacred as prayer, as essential to the spirit as food to the body. It is our creative work that reveals us to ourselves and allows us to transform our experience and imagination into new forms, forms that reflect to us in a language of symbol who we are, what we are becoming, what we have loved and feared. This is the alchemy of creation: that as my energy fuses with the Source of energy, a newness rises in the shape of who I am and I myself am altered in the course of its release.

I am never the same in the wake of this work. As I create, I come into my power and wisdom, into my deeper knowing, into that newness that becomes the gift I share with the world. As a result of the time I spend at my work, there is more of me to give—more awareness, more joy, more depth. I become centered in the process, focused on the interior, attuned to the inner voice. Life is no longer about time and demands and errands. It is about the extraordinary metamorphosis of one thing into another. What begins as cocoon emerges as butterfly. What once was sorrow may now be song.

And as I am changed by the art that passes through me in the process of becoming, so am I changed by the creations of others. Having read your poem, mine will contain it and add to its truth. Having felt the cold of your cobalt blue, my red will remember and its voice will be sharper. In the stroke of your brush, the wail of your cello, I find fragments of myself I have long forgotten. In your photographs and sculptures, I find my passions mirrored, my visions revived.

My walls are covered with creations that move me and help me remember the whole I am part of. When I awake in the morning, my eyes focus first on a photograph of polar bears dancing in the snow. It is in that instant I feel my bear-ness, that need to hibernate, to romp through nature, to hunt and search for that which feeds me. The image enters into me, allows me to understand more clearly, more symbolically, the life I am living and attempting to create.

Throughout my house are portraits of strong and powerful women — old women, dancing women, women together, women isolated and alone — all from cultures outside my own and each in its way reflecting me and my oneness with her. I'm healed by these images, comforted and encouraged, for where they have journeyed it is safe for me to go.

It is the same with music — there is something for every need, to be chosen from the stack for comfort, inspiration, dance, meditation, celebration. And on my bookshelves are works that have changed my life, altered my consciousness, led to journeys to far-off places and inner worlds — novels, poems, nonfiction, screenplays, each adding essential ingredients to who I am and what I am becoming.

What others have created has shaped my life, and I am moved by the power of these works every day, conscious of the obstacles that each artist faced in the process of birthing them. And I think if these artists reckoned with their fears, their lack of time, their feelings of inadequacy and still went forward, then so can I.

For it is the same with all of us — we have our terrors, our doubts, our cultures that negate the work of the spirit. And yet we continue, journeying inward to find what is there that seeks release and offers comfort. Over and over we transmute one thing into another, turning tragedies and triumphs into sculpture, dance, novels, boldstroke paintings, and heartrending operas, all conjured in our private hours and offered to the whole like food for the soul, a wrap against the chill.

The call to create is a calling like no other, a voice within that howls for expression, shadow longing to merge with light. It is an act of faith to respond to that voice, to give it our time, and in return, if grace be with us, we are blessed with a piece that can be of use, a piece that has light and a life of its own. One honest poem can spark a revolution, one play thaw a frozen heart. And who knows what works have been inspired by Michelangelo's *David*, O'Keeffe's paintings, Rodin's sculptures? What one of us conjures inspires another.

For there is power in the work we are moved to create — prophetic power, redemptive power. Art that emerges from our inward journeys is a revealing art, a tale-telling mirror that collapses time and expands dimension. Our creations contain the past and the future, the known and the unknown, the breath of spirit and the flesh of politic. As we respond to the world we are part of, what we create adds to its essence, changes its shape, heals its wounds.

No matter what the medium, art reveals us to ourselves and heightens the level of human consciousness. I find myself in another's poem, see myself in another's image, become more myself through another's unfolding. Art is a mirror not only to the soul of the artist, but to the whole of civilization that celebrates its creation.

We as creators hold in our bones the lessons of history, the paths to the future. The lines we draw are lifelines, lines that connect, lines that hold the contours of the ages to come. It is up to us — those who know that urge to create, who have felt the tug of that inner voice — to create the world we want to be a part of, to release the words we want to inspire us.

Simone Weil once wrote, "The work of art which I do not make, none other will ever make it." It is up to us, to you and me, to heal ourselves and by that, the world. So let us give our time to the work that heals, to that creative journey that will lead us home.

And in the moments when we are fragile, forgetting our gifts, forgetting the power of our creative works, let us return to this creed and call forth the Muse:

Artist's Creed

I believe I am worth the time it takes to create
whatever I feel called to create.

I believe that my work is worthy of its own space,
which is worthy of the name Sacred.

I believe that, when I enter this space, I have the right
to work in silence, uninterrupted, for as long as I choose.

I believe that the moment I open myself
to the gifts of the Muse,
I open myself to the Source of All Creation
and become One with the Mother of Life Itself.

I believe that my work is joyful, useful
and constantly changing,
flowing through me like a river with no
beginning and no end.

I believe that what it is I am called to do
will make itself known when I have made myself ready.

I believe that the time I spend creating my art
is as precious as the time I spend giving to others.

I believe that what truly matters in the making of art
is not what the final piece looks like or sounds like,
not what it is worth or not worth, but what
newness gets added to the universe in the process
of the piece itself becoming.

I believe that I am not alone in my attempts
to create, and that once I begin the work,
settle into the strangeness,
the words will take shape, the form find life,
and the spirit take flight.

I believe that as the Muse gives to me,
so does she deserve from me:
faith, mindfulness, and enduring commitment.

✳

Jan Phillips is an award-winning writer, photographer, video producer and workshop director. She is the author of *Marry Your Muse: Making a Lasting Commitment to Your Creativity* (Quest Books, 1997), *Making Peace: One Woman's Journey Around the World* (Friendship Press, 1990), and the forthcoming *God is at Eye Level — Photography as a Healing Art.* Her work has appeared in the *New York Times, Ms. Magazine,* the *Christian Science Monitor, Utne Reader, Texas Highways, National Catholic Reporter*, and dozens of regional magazines and newspapers. She has won awards for outstanding writing and photography from the New York Press Association, National Organization for Women, National Catholic Press Association, National Federation of Press Women, National Religious Press Association, and the Syracuse Press Club.

She is a cofounder of Syracuse Cultural Workers, publishers and distributors of artwork for social justice; was editor of its annual Women Artists' Datebook *In Praise of the Muse*; and has been a social activist for twenty-five years. In a one-woman tour around the world, she presented slideshows on the U.S. peace movement to more than 6,000 people in twenty-two countries. She conducts workshops around the country on creativity.

Words from the Marrow

JOHN FOX

More than a mode of perception,
poetry is above all a way of life, of integral life.

— St. John Perse
Nobel Prize 1960

The sudden writing of a poem by someone in grief, some-one unsure of which path to take, or someone deeply affected by the suffering of another suggests that writing poems is, at essence, a spontaneous, creative action connected to the healing process. A cry in the belly or a flash of memory glimpsed in the heart may compel us to make poems. These things can evoke our attention and, in our desire to heal, ignite our creativity.

This experience is more common than we may acknowl-edge. On any morning at two A.M., someone is awake, unable to sleep, trying to release a feeling of distress and find words for the unspeakable.

. . . my

jaws ache for release, for
             words that will say

anything. I force myself
              to remember
who I am, what I am, and
              why I am here. . . .

— Phillip Levine

Ruth Stone's poem *Advice* implores us to not only say *something*, but to discern and speak up for what we need.

Dear Children, you must try to say
Something when you are in need.
Don't confuse hunger with greed,
And don't wait until you are dead.

Acts of discernment, insights regarding what is true for you, are energized by the action of writing. You illuminate something previously known only in shadow. By writing, you give life to what matters, you give shape to what you know. You find your voice. As the homeless muse (played by poet Amiri Baraka) in Warren Beatty's film *Bulworth* kept imploring, "Be a spirit! Don't be a ghost!"

Poetry is both creative and healing because it helps us to recognize ourselves spiritually and to give this recognition expression. The poet Gwendolyn Brooks said it so simply: "The poetry is myself." We turn to poem making to reclaim who and what we are.

The word "reclaim," comes from the Latin word *reclamare*. It literally means "to cry out." A poem enables us to embody our voice, to "get physical" by giving our inner voice the shape of words.

Expressive and evocative qualities are inherent in the spoken word, qualities of language that permit us to sense, know, and feel the connection between our innermost reality and the circumstances of the world in which we live.

> *It is with words we begin*
> *to know where we are,*
> *the details of existence*
> *reveal our code of connection*

> — Kimberley Nelson

In her poem "Saying Things," Marilyn Krysl shows us what is possible when we enter into the playful, delicious, and intimate act of speaking a word:

> *This is a birthday party for the mouth — it's better than ice*
> *   cream,*
> *say waterlily, refrigerator, hartbeest, Prussian blue,*
> *and the word will take you, if you let it,*
> *the word will take you along across the air of your head*
> *so that you're there as it settles into the thing it was made for,*

adding to it a shimmer and the bird song of its sound,
sound that comes from you, the hand letting go
its dove, yours the mouth speaking the thing into
　　existence, . . .

Poetry is often called "the language of the soul." The word "poet," in fact, comes from *poesis*, or "one who makes": that is, your mouth speaking the thing into existence! Poem making can connect us with a primordial core, something close to the bone and perhaps to the Divine. We discover that we are expansive spirits instead of hungry ghosts.

Sitting in a restaurant one evening, I sank deeply into this connection, into my longing to be at-one with things. I remember searching my heart to feel the interrelationship between the evocative and expressive aspects of my life. For instance, between being alive on earth and the wonder of the stars, I wrote,

THERE IS AN ORIGIN
For each true poem there is an origin:
Blessed ignorance of words that turn
To splendid fire, as stars in space will yearn
To find on earth their upstretched twin.

Words can allow you to enter the creative center of your life. In that space something is aflame with the desire to express itself — and to reveal the link between the core of a star and the very marrow of your bones. Like T cells made inside your bone marrow and received into your blood stream, a poem comes into being on the page or through your voice and has the capacity to creatively apply itself to protect, enhance, and expand your whole being.

The act of writing creatively, of working on words so they say what you mean and so the words do their work upon you, is similar to the action of your immune system responding to heal a wound or disease, maintaining wholeness and encouraging optimum well-being. The healing action of poetry reveals something essential and unique about who you are and how you are related to the world you live in, and this creative process both cleanses and invigorates.

Poems celebrate, rant, give joy, express anguish; they speak uncomfortable and awkward truths; they tackle hard questions and issues without finding answers — and sometimes, they reveal life-changing insights, such as the stunning and simple awareness that you are already whole. If you want to discover how poetry offers wholeness — a connection to something deep and inclusive within yourself and the world — become aware of qualities in a poem that give writing more life force:

- How a poem connects your imagination to the world, often through detail

- How a poem has the capacity to contain emotional paradox

- How a poem releases feeling onto the page through your distinct voice — translating for the reader what grieves, troubles, or encourages you, or what gives you joy

- How a poem surprises you with something you did not
  know before you wrote or read the poem

Imagination, detail, paradox, feeling, voice, and surprise —
each is intimately connected to the meaning and wholeness we
experience — or don't experience — in our lives. In his poem "A
Ritual to Read to Each Other," William Stafford draws attention
to the voice within:

And so I appeal to a voice, to something shadowy,
a remote important region in all who talk:
though we could fool each other, we should consider —
lest the parade of our mutual life get lost in the dark.

For someone in crisis, the capacity to allow this "remote
important region" a chance to speak may help that person live
with paradox. How do I live when someone I love has died? Why
do I love someone so much who has been so difficult?

Emotional opposites often pressure us to explain something
logically. Our inner voices, however, are not limited to logical
explanations or linear thinking. Our poetic voices are willing to
not know and to give us the precious time we need to feel, listen,
and wait.

Your unique, creative voice is especially nourished by atten-
tive listening. Nick Penna wrote these lines at age eleven:

If you can listen you find
answers to questions you didn't know.

John Keats called this capacity to feel, listen, and wait when much is unknown "negative capability," a state when someone "is capable of being in uncertainties, Mysteries, doubts, without any irritable reaching after fact and reason. . . ." Keats thought that Shakespeare possessed a genius for this creative capacity. Nick Penna seems to understand the wisdom of feeling and waiting, too.

But don't despair that you are no Shakespeare or Nick Penna! Life's challenges to our equilibrium and resilience do not wait on literary genius or the spontaneous wisdom of childhood; harsh and difficult experiences may compel us, whoever and at whatever age we are, to find our unique creative responses to uncertainties and doubts when fact or reason won't do.

Writing a poem is like focusing on that spot on the wall my gym teacher taught me to look at when I learned to balance on the balance beam. Her goal was to help me discover and trust the simple wisdom of my body in order to find my center.

Pouring focus into and working closely with the images and sounds of a poem can also help you draw on your centering wisdom. Your concentration on poem making can reveal insights that bring a much deeper balance and joy than you may achieve by reaching outside yourself for the "right" answer.

A poem can hold a paradox steady before you so that your inner voice can shed light on your experience. Hearing that voice may allow your imagination to lead you forward, gradually, to find a sense of wholeness, even with a torn heart or while travelling through a dark passage of your life.

Donna Kennedy has been a journalist for twenty-five years.

She writes sensitively about human potential for the features section of her newspaper. Donna enjoyed poetry, in an occasional way, but felt no particular desire to write poems. It was her mother's death that stirred her to write:

RITUAL
For seven days after my mother died,
I slept in her bed and sipped her wine.
Her long black dress fit me, so I wore it.
I patted my cheeks with her makeup
and smeared red lipstick on my mouth
like a child playing dress-up.

After seven days, I scattered her ashes
and returned to my house,
surprised to find her face in my mirror.

Donna's poem distills and condenses imagination, detail, paradox, feeling, voice, and, profoundly in the last line, surprise. "Ritual" *contains* her experience, so she has time to feel it. She acknowledges her loss by *sensing* her experience and then describing it with detail in a very intimate way. Donna can look at her poem, then set it aside, then return to it and refine it or reflect on it — allowing new feelings and insights to emerge. Writing this poem allows Donna to evoke and express, distill and condense, reflect and integrate.

Writing or reflecting on your poem is not the only way to allow poetry to affect and even change your life. Reading a poem by another poet at the right time can both heal emotional wounds and ignite your creative response. So it was for me when I was twenty-five — several years after the amputation of my right leg — and read the following lines by Greek poet Odysseus Elytis, winner of the Nobel prize for literature. His poem spoke to me like nothing else:

. . . My friend, when night wakens your electric grief
I see the tree of the heart spreading
Your arms open beneath a pure idea
To which you call
But which will not descend
For years and years:
It up there and you down here.

And yet longing's vision awakens flesh one day
And there where only bare solitude once shone,
A city now laughs lovely as you would have it
You almost see it, it is waiting for you
Give me your hand so that we may go there before the Dawn
Floods it with cries of triumph
Give me your hand — before birds gather
On the shoulders of men to announce in song
That Virginal Hope is seen coming at last
Out of the distant sea.

We will go together, and let them stone us
And let them say we walk with our heads in the clouds —

Those who have never felt, my friend,
With what iron, what stones, what blood, what fire,
We build, dream and sing.

Elytis's words eased my pain more than painkillers did. This special poem became a catalyst and companion for my breaking through self-imposed limitations. Longing finally awakened my flesh and bones — I decided to run a marathon.

Training for a few years to run on a prosthesis brought fire and blood and singing to me. The marathon was a tremendous effort and a joy to accomplish, but the final gift of the poem and of running was more lasting. I made space in my life for both grief and joy. I realized the deep, creative well I could draw from. The poem and running evoked hope I could trust.

Six years after running the marathon, I wrote to Elytis in Athens. I told him my marathon story and sent him some of my poems. He wrote back on an old typewriter: "A window to the unknown but also the true has been opened to you. And it will help you."

What remarkable words about the unknown's relationship to my writing: "It will help you." I have come to sense that the most healing and creative aspect of poetry (and of life itself) is this: it can open us to accept help from the unknown — and also from the true.

People who have not written much poetry, who feel they don't compare to "real" poets, can in fact do deep work and make creative strides by writing. Their poems can speak truths in ways that change their lives and reveal new worlds. One of my students wrote the following poem early in our writing circle:

UNDERNEATH
What language can't reach
is so much.
The hook dangles
from the fishline,
while the fish
swim by.
The sea urchins
are un-interested,
the kelp waves,
a whole world
expands.
The hook finds
a few slender
words,
pulls them
to light.
Maybe I
can cook them.

— Barbara McEnerney

Barbara shows a willingness to wait, listen, and feel. The last two lines suggest creative hope. She allows for the possibility that writing may lead to something more, something meaningful. *How* we listen to our poetic voices and those of others affects our capacity to liberate this meaning and refine our creativity.

Mindful listening can teach us to wait to receive what holds meaning. When we write from our experiences and blend it with listening, we create an openness to receive guidance and learn from what lies just beyond consciousness.

We see such openness in the spontaneous know-how displayed by someone maneuvering a whitewater raft, and we have also experienced it through the guiding and intuitive logic we receive in a dream. Our openness to poem making is informed by sensitive, moment-by-moment awareness and by a letting go that allows us to receive that flow of awareness with freshness.

Barbara kept writing after she wrote" "Underneath." Some months later she wrote a poem about her father. She is discovering her relationship with poetic language. She is growing to trust her process of writing:

WHAT HOLDS
Enormous space is near
even when I walk
through a Target store
with my father
to find him a new belt.
We had just left
St. Mary's Cemetery —
a visit to his parents' gravesites.
I watched my father
sit down on the grass
of his own grave.
His belt was frayed,
held by one thin leather cord.

In Target we bought
him a sturdy one.
My brother and I
wrapped it around him.
My father joked
about flunking his army
class in night navigation
back in the 1940s.
In the huge Target store
he felt lost. He said,
"You can't even navigate
by the stars in here."
I felt enormous space
spread and deepen.

This poem followed Barbara's earlier poems about the complex relationship she has with her father. Yet, what she discovers in this poem is a deep desire to protect and love him, the poignancy of change and death, and a realization about "what holds." She found in her words something to cook as food for her soul.

Poem making joins the realms of sensation, feeling, thought, and soul. These aspects of ourselves, so often relegated to ill-fitting compartments, are capable, through poetry, of communicating with one another in ways that can be healing, utterly frank, life affirming, spontaneous, inclusive, and revelatory. Particulars of our experiences are door frames through which we enter deeper relationships. Sacred words are kept in those thresholds — the life-giving power of our own words.

✳

JOHN FOX is a poet and a certified poetry therapist. He teaches in the Graduate School of Psychology at John F. Kennedy University in Orinda, California, and in the California Poets in the Schools program. Fox offers workshops at Esalen and Omega Institutes and throughout the United States. He is the author of the widely acclaimed *Finding What You Didn't Lose: Expressing Your Truth and Creativity Through Poem-Making* (Tarcher/Putnam, 1995) and *Poetic Medicine: The Healing Art of Poem-Making* (Tarcher/Putnam, 1997). He is the recipient of the National Association for Poetry Therapy's 1995 Distinguished Service Award. He lives in Mountain View, California.

Writer and Witness, Healing Through Story

CHRISTINA BALDWIN

When a new child is born in the family,
the ancestors gather above it and whisper
among themselves:
*"Maybe this will be the one who tells our stories
and heals our lineage."*

— Angeles Arrien

*I*t is usually evening. People have come from far away, flown into a city and then driven to a comfortable retreat tucked somewhere in the surrounding countryside. We have said hello, unpacked in bare rooms, and nestled in. We've had supper and have begun social conversations discovering who we are. Now, the first council is called.

I have arranged the seating in a circle. There is a shawl spread in the center space, on the floor or on a low coffee table. There is a seven-day candle — a cylinder of glass, paraffin, and wick, that

I order from a Catholic supply house. It will serve as our eternal flame, the light on the hearth, the reminder of campfire, and a tradition of story that trails behind us for thousands of years. We are the ones in our families and communities who seem to make sense of life through speaking and writing our histories as our lives unfold — journal writers, letter writers, readers. We have been laughing at supper sharing anecdotes; now there is a quiet expectancy as we come into the softly lit room that will house us in our collective time.

People enter the circle with arms full of belongings and longings. They settle in soft chairs surrounded by small piles of what they have carried this far to share. They bring satchels full of loose papers, old letters, years of journals, pens, blank tablets, sometimes a laptop computer, photographs, and other mementos that invoke a particular time and incident they feel compelled to weave into story as artfully as they can. They are like birds nesting, a diverse rookery of different feathers.

I am sitting with them, the caller of this circle, and here is what I bring: forty years of journal writing and my belief that story shapes the psyche and frames what we attempt with our precious lives; fifteen years of teaching this class; and several decades' experience calling people into this form of gathering — the form of the circle.

In this circle creativity is tapped and wells up, bubbles and gushes and dries up and is found again. The circle creates a collective container that can hold each person's creative process and provides a community of witnesses to listen to the resulting stories. Writers in a ring, we sit at the intersecting point where the solitary nature of writing and the collective nature of witnessing meet. This is ancient ground.

We of the human tribe originated from this place: gathering at the end of the day's journey, bringing bounty to share — a haunch of meat, a handful of roots and nuts, a tale to barter for a place at the fire. And we have lost this place: obliterated it with bright lights and noise, the incessant background drone of media and machinery that permeate the neatly isolated shelters most of us retreat to. We do not know what our neighbors are having for dinner, nor do we share it with them. And we certainly don't know their stories. We don't even know our own stories . . . and that is why we have come: to reclaim the stories that shape our lives.

When we are still, I light the candle: This is where story began, I remind us. Two things will occur that will provide a depth of healing we are only partially cognizant of in this moment of gathering. First, the class lessons and the writing exercises will help each of us discover a nugget of personal truth that is still buried in us as we enter the circle. I sense this nugget waiting in myself as well as in the others, some piece of story that will give me an insight that is both personal and universal. I have been waking at night watching dream images scamper out of reach. I have been staring into the woods while bicycling the backroads that surround my home, seeing something flit into the trees. I have been crying out on the pages of my journal: give me my story! There is a lump in my throat, a

sore place over my heart, a tightness in my belly I have learned
to see as the roaming of the nugget inside me, like old shrapnel
working its way to the surface. I still have BBs in my knee from
the time Leland Kersey mistook me for a rabbit when I was five
years old. Our most universal stories are something like this —
a bit of history under our skin, often a wounding, that is ready
to be transformed.

And then, at the end of the week, when we read what we
have written, we will speak this truth into the circle and it will
be held with compassion and understanding. One by one we
will take the awesome risk of telling, afraid no one will see anything except an old BB, meaningless except to ourselves, afraid
we will not be believed, afraid we will be scorned and sent
away from the fire. Simply afraid. And yet by telling we will
have the opportunity to look into the eyes of our listeners and
discover acceptance, notice the Divine residing within the faces
of those who have heard us. We will have a moment of grace
when our lives are held in a sacred manner and the group bows
down before each one's story. And we will be forever changed.

As the writing teacher I will lecture and lead discussions on
forms of creative nonfiction, on metaphor and reality, on time
and tension and other topics, but my deepest role is to serve as
guardian of this circle — to weave the container and see that it
maintains the tensile strength and open-heartedness we will all
need to call upon. To prepare our readiness to both speak and
listen, we make certain agreements up front. No one is asked to
take the risk of revealment until everyone present has agreed
to hold this experience with respect and shared responsibility.

I call these agreements the Four Ancient Laws of the Fire:

1. We agree that what is said in the circle belongs to the circle and is not shared without permission.
2. We volunteer to listen to one another with discernment and not judgment.
3. We promise to each ask for what we need and offer what we can.
4. When we have lost our way or need to rest in the process, we agree to become silent and wait for further guidance.

After we agree to abide by these laws, the woman on my left speaks her name, puts a smooth stone, a garden trowel, and the first story into the center.* "Ten years ago," she begins, "I ran away from home, headed east in my car leaving a note on the kitchen table asking my husband to feed the cat and fend for himself and our remaining teenager, that I just had to get far enough away to have some thoughts of my very own. Three days later I came to the Atlantic Ocean and stopped. It was the bravest thing I ever did and had tremendous consequences for myself, my husband, our children — even the cat. I have talked to people about this turning point, but never gotten down to the level of story I know it deserves. I'm here this week as a digger. This trowel reminds me to dig down until I hit the real story. This rock is my touchstone from the beach."

The next person places a photograph in the center: a faded snapshot of a little boy wrapped around the pants leg of a man

* The stories shared here have been altered to honor the Four Laws or are used with permission.

visible in the picture only as far as his waist. The man's hands are jammed in his pockets. "My dad died last year and I found this photo in his desk drawer. I always felt his distance, the choice he made in this moment to keep his hands in his pockets when I longed to feel them on my shoulders." The storyteller wipes his eyes, then goes on. "I don't remember this instance, but the fact that he saved the picture all these years is intriguing to me. He's dead, but not gone. I'm here because I want a way to discover him, to find his heart and how it connects to my heart, to bring us into better relationship."

And so it goes around the ring. We enter the alchemy of writing — and have the chance to spin lead into gold. The magic for me is that coming into the ring we each assume that so much of our lives is lead: dross, dull, uninteresting; but as we work with our skills to vivify detail and unpack the moment, gold flashes at the bottom of the pan. This transformation is due partly to the time spent writing, honing the skills to paint with words, and equally to the time spent reading aloud and listening to one another. Others are often the first to inform us when we are on the motherlode of a story.

One stunning example of how the soul of creativity is fostered by this combination is the story of Susan. Susan arrived at the writing circle struggling with cancer and looking for ways to explore the spiritual dimensions of her illness. Bald and pale from the ravages of treatment, she checked in by saying, "In the past three years I have lost everything about myself that is female. I have no breasts, no uterus, no ovaries, no hair. It is hard not to take this as a personal attack. First I thought God was attacking me, but now I wonder if I'm attacking myself. I don't know how long I have to live. I'm through whining and badgering and screaming unfair, now I just want a story that helps me make peace with myself. And so I've come to write and write and write until I find it."

As touched as we were by her story, we couldn't provide her any answers. She brought a photograph of herself at age six and another at age eight and put them in the center. The contrast was shocking. "What happened to you?" I asked her later. "Look at the difference in your face, your stance. At age six you exude confidence, an attitude of 'look out world here I come.' At age eight, you look as though your spirit had been run over by a truck."

"Oh, it wasn't me who got run over," she said, "but a little boy in the neighborhood who did — Tommy Campbell."

"Were you friends?"

"I don't remember much about it, except it seemed to cast a pall over all the mothers and therefore all the children."

"Why don't you see what you can reconstruct," I suggested. "It's no accident that I used getting run over as a metaphor, and you picked up a real memory."

Susan made a writing nest where she spent the afternoon: pillows to comfort her bony joints, a lit candle by the photo of herself at six, and a magazine photo of a freckled boy. "Okay, kids," she invited these images, "tell me your stories." She entered a writing dream, and this is what she saw: walking home from school one day in first grade she was on one side of her small-town street and Tommy, her classmate, was on the other side. A verbal bantering began between them. He teased and flirted, threatening to kiss her. She flirted back, "Oh yeah? Well if you want to kiss me, you'll have to catch me first!" She stood with her hands on her hips, confident that she was desirable. Tommy laughed — equally confident — and darted into the street without looking. He was struck by a car and killed. As all these pieces came together in her mind she wept with freshened grief. That evening we all wept, listening to the raw dialog she had written between those two long-gone children and the remembrances that had emerged from her writing session.

We listened without intruding on her chain reaction of insight as pieces of her story were stringing themselves together. "No wonder I've lost all my female organs. . . . No wonder I never had a date until I moved away to college. . . . Guilty, guilty, guilty . . ." she intoned quietly.

I carefully leaned forward. "May I ask you something?" She nodded. "You cannot change the past, but you can change the story you've made out of the past. What completely different assumption could you make about that moment that would change all your other assumptions?"

"I don't know. I was only six years old."

"Yes, and the guilt and confusion of the adults swirled around you, filling you with feelings no one ever named. Take their reactions out of it. Just go back and write out what happened between you and Tommy. Write out what happened between your souls. . . ."

That night Susan wrote her way to healing. She had always

assumed it was the boy's death she carried inside, but her writing let her see that all these years she had carried his life. "He's always been with me," she cried sweetly, after reading in our next listening circle. "He's not angry. He's not sad. He has served willingly as my inner champion. Before I got sick, I worked in a very male business. Maybe it was Tommy who helped me hold my own. How lucky I've been. I wish I'd known it."

"Which version of this story is true?" students ask me when I share it. "Do we have to choose?" I ask in return. "Perhaps both versions are real. They are flip sides of each other. Guilt and grace cannot be separated. When there is the need for grace, aren't guilt and confusion present?"

What matters most to me is that the story worked its alchemy and served as an instrument of healing. What matters is that a community sat with one another in a moment of revelation and witnessed one member's ability to change her story from guilt ridden to grace filled. And then they sat with the next person and the next and let revelations occur around the ring. And though she died within the next year, Susan fulfilled the charge she had brought to class — to make peace with herself.

It is usually evening. People have come a long way. We enter the circle with arms full of belongings and longings. And if we can hold the intersection point where the solitary nature of writing and the collective nature of listening meet, we can fulfill the whisper of the ancestors and heal our lineage with story.

✳

CHRISTINA BALDWIN is cofounder, with Ann Linnea, of PeerSpirit circling, a practical methodology for community building and spirit-centered meeting and action. Their understanding of the need and applications of the circle is the theme of Baldwin's most recent book, *Calling the Circle: The First and Future Culture* (Bantam Doubleday Dell, 1998). She is also one of the foundational writers and leaders in a 25-year revival in personal writing through her two classic books on journal keeping: *One to One: Self-Understanding Through Journal Writing* (M. Evans, 1997) and *Life's Companion: Journal Writing as a Spiritual Quest* (Bantam Doubleday Dell, 1990). Christina Baldwin may be contacted for speeches, workshops, and facilitation through PeerSpirit at (360) 331-3580 or through her website: www.peerspirit.com.

Creativity and Social Healing

RIANE EISLER, J.D.

What is creativity? Is it merely innovation, something new? Or does creativity have another, more intrinsic meaning, as in the distinction between creating and destroying? These are fundamental questions in an age when new discoveries about how genes are put together are leading to technological innovation such as genetic engineering, an age when the discovery of how atoms can be split led to atom bombs and the horrors of Hiroshima and Nagasaki.

If we are to find answers to these urgent questions, we have to take a fresh look at issues that at first glance may not seem related. These include questions about what kinds of values and social arrangements we have been taught to consider normal and important, and how the roles and relations of the two halves of humanity have been structured.

When most people think of creativity, they think of men such as Michelangelo or Einstein. Women such as the Nobel-prize-winning chemist Barbara McClintock and the pioneering Renaissance painter Sofonisba Anguissola come less readily to mind, even though they had to have enormous fortitude and courage to overcome the obstacles that barred them from the arts and sciences. Most of us are also taught to differentiate between arts and crafts, between high culture and low culture. And characteristically, the arts and high culture are areas dominated by men; the crafts and low culture are areas where women have been allowed to work.

Some may say that although this differentiation has clearly been a problem for women, it has not been of much social consequence. In fact, however, the exclusion of women from the arts, sciences, politics, and other areas of the so-called public sphere has had a profound effect on social values and priorities. Moreover, the gendered classification of what is and is not a creative domain has effectively reinforced a gendered conception of what is and is not important. In the process, it has also maintained the devaluation of socially essential activities stereotypically associated with women, activities such as caring for others and creating and maintaining a healthy and aesthetically pleasing home environment, while deflecting the support for creativity from these areas. At the same time, it has channeled social and financial support for activities stereotypically associated with men rather than with women, such as weaponry and warfare.

This has not been good for either men or women. Moreover, these stereotypes have nothing to do with anything inherent in women or men. As my work and that of many other investigators show, gender roles and relations are culturally constructed to a much larger extent than is generally believed.

We are here dealing with gender roles and relations appropri-ate for a particular social system: one orienting primarily to what I have in my research identified as a dominator rather than a partnership model of society. And it is precisely this kind of social system that today threatens our very survival.

SOCIAL SYSTEMS, CREATIVITY, AND OUR LIVES

As the term implies, the dominator model structures rela-tions in terms of rigid hierarchies of domination, ranking men over women, race over race, religion over religion, and humans over nature. In the dominator model, power is viewed as power over. It is the power symbolized by the blade: the life-threaten-ing power to maintain control through fear and force. The part-nership model is, by contrast, much more egalitarian. Here, as we see from archaeological excavations of the Minoan civiliza-tion that flourished on the island of Crete approximately 3,500 years ago, there is no great social investment in maintaining domination through fear and force. Here hierarchies are what I have called hierarchies of actualization rather than of domina-tion. Here power is viewed in a way we hear more about today: power to. Its essence is the power to create, nurture, and illu-minate life symbolized by the chalice or holy grail — a metaphor for the life-giving womb of the Great Goddess of ancient times.

The Minoan civilization was an extraordinarily creative civ-ilization. The art of this more partnership-oriented civilization has been called by scholars "unique in the annals of civiliza-tion" for its love of life and nature. Moreover, although the

Minoans are noted for their beautiful frescoes, sculptures, and other fine arts, they also expressed their creativity in more contextualized ways, with much attention paid to creativity in making daily life more comfortable and aesthetically pleasing. Greek archaeologist Nicolas Platon writes that the influence of women and of what he terms a feminine sensitivity is evidenced in every sphere. In contrast to the sharp divisions between haves and have-nots and masters and slaves of other ancient high civilizations, Minoan Crete was also not a slave society. Rather, it had what Platon describes as a remarkably high general standard of living. In addition, the Minoans were the great traders of their day, selling their beautiful crafts far and wide (for example, the fine Minoan pottery found in Egypt) rather than, like more dominator-oriented ancient civilizations, acquiring wealth largely through armed conquest.

In short, human inventiveness is channeled very differently in societies that orient to either the partnership or the dominator model. Societies that conform more to the partnership model invest heavily in improving both material and spiritual life, as evidenced in human welfare and enlightenment. Societies that conform closely to the dominator model make much more of an investment in what I call technologies of destruction rather than in technologies of production, reproduction, conservation, and actualization, with critical implications for all aspects of culture and of life.

Here once again we come back to gender: to how the cultural construction of the roles and relations of the male and female halves of humanity is inextricably interconnected with all aspects of life and particularly to what is and is not socially valued and supported. And we also come back to the peculiar definitions of creativity we have inherited from times that oriented more closely to the dominator model.

For example, women generally have had the responsibility to nurture children, which requires a great deal of both planned and improvisational creativity and which is certainly an extremely important task. Yet, although this and other "domestic" activities have often been overidealized, they have also been undervalued and certainly have not conventionally been classified as creative. Cooking tasty and nutritious meals also requires a great deal of both planned and improvised creativity and is again a very important task. Yet it has rarely been valued as an artistic creation when done by women, no matter how beautifully presented, whereas chefs (traditionally males) have been viewed as culinary artists.

As we continue to reexamine creativity from this new perspective, we also see that many of women's creative activities have been relational, for example, cooking a meal, decorating a house, embellishing a utilitarian object such as a quilt (a contemporary remnant of women's traditional role in weaving and in making clothes for the family). In other words, they have been directed toward making the life of others more comfortable or aesthetically pleasing — again a very important task.

By no longer associating creativity only with the domains and activities in the public sphere stereotypically assigned to men as a group, we not only revalue what have historically been domains of women's creativity, but we enlarge our horizons about creativity itself. Most important, we change the definition of what is and is not creative and what is and is not important. In particular, we begin to apply creativity to where we most need it: our daily lives.

INVENTIVENESS, CREATIVITY, AND OUR FUTURE

Not only is what women do considered less important than what men do in societies orienting to the dominator model, but also male activities that do not conform to stereotypes of masculinity are devalued. For much of recorded Western history, when society still oriented far more to the dominator model, the only acceptable career for noblemen was the military. One result of this association of manliness with domination and violence was the view (still lingering in our time) that gentler men and boys are effeminate, as illustrated by derogatory terms such as "sissy" or "weak sister." Still another result, reflected in the lingering social ambivalence about artists, is that in this stereotypical kind of thinking artists are considered effete or effeminate.

Looked at from this perspective, the fact that creativity is today increasingly valued can be seen as an important sign of movement toward a more partnership-oriented society. So also can the entry of more women into traditionally male domains, a consequence of which is that more and more women are being counted as creative, including a growing number of Nobel prize winners. And still another sign of movement toward a partnership social and ideological organization is that as women have risen in status, so has the stereotypically feminine, so that the very definition of creativity (whether it is by men or by women) is today being broadened to include its social and relational dimensions.

In this connection, it is interesting that women's creativity has often been a group activity, for example working together in the kitchen. Moreover, and this is a critical point, women's creativity has often been contextual; that is, it has provided the nurturing context for the creativity of others as, for example, when a mother encourages a child's first attempts to create words or draw. In fact, often women's creativity has itself been contextualized: unlike a painting or a sculpture we may see once a year in a museum, it cannot be abstracted from its context, but is rather part of the texture of our lives.

But if we are to complete this shift toward a partnership way of structuring society — which is countered by enormous opposition and periodic regressions — we need much more channeling of creativity to develop social and economic inventions appropriate for partnership living. Fortunately, there is already movement in this healing direction, not only by individual artists using their work to raise the consciousness of our interconnection with one another and our natural habitat, but also by organizations working for a more equitable, peaceful, and humane future. For example, the Alliance for a Caring Economy is developing and publicizing ways of recognizing and rewarding the urgently needed caretaking activities that keep society going — activities that have stereotypically been associated with women and hence devalued. This also means creating ways of providing far more economic and social support for the work of environmental housekeeping — of keeping our planet healthy and pollution free. It also means developing social and economic inventions in both the market and nonmarket economies to highly reward caring for children, whether it is performed by women or men.

Caretaking and caring is the most foundationally creative human work. Hence, the new contextualized, gender-holistic approach to creativity I have proposed makes an even more fundamental distinction: the differentiation between creativity and inventiveness. For example, the creation of a clean bomb, which kills only people but leaves property untouched, can be described as inventive but not creative. The Nazis' innovations in methods of mass extermination can be seen not as creativity, but as destructive inventiveness.

As I have suggested elsewhere, the term creativity, rather than just inventiveness, should be reserved for ideas and activities that support, nurture, and illuminate our lives, activities, and ideas. Such ideas increase rather than limit the choices open to our children, ourselves, and our communities. It should not be applied to the development of technologies that kill or to the development of better means of dominating, exploiting, or limiting the choices available to us. I cite, for example, genetically engineered sterile seeds that are today being marketed by agro-monopolies with no concern for possible consequences, and human bioengineering that presents even more serious risks to our future.

This distinction between creativity and inventiveness makes it possible to introduce the element of ethical judgment into discussions of creativity, which is urgently needed if we are to have a healthy soul. Then, in contrast to inventiveness, which can be soulless and even evil, creativity has a soul.

SELECTED REFERENCES

Alliance for a Caring Economy. A project of the Center for Partnership Studies, P.O. Box 51936, Pacific Grove, CA 93950. (webpage: www.partnershipway.org).

Global Futures Foundation, 801 Crocker Road, Sacramento, CA 95864. (webpage: www.globalff.org; E-mail: wbpratt@aol.com).

Riane Eisler, *The Chalice and the Blade: Our History, Our Future* (San Francisco: Harper & Row, 1987).

———— "Cultural Transformation Theory: A New Paradigm for History," in *Macrohistory and Macrohistorians*, eds., Johan Galtung and Sohail Inayatullah (Westport,Connecticut: Praeger, 1997).

———— "Partnership and the Arts," Concept Paper of Center for Partnership Studies (1988).

———— *Sacred Pleasure: Sex, Myth, and the Politics of the Body* (San Francisco: HarperSanFrancisco, 1995).

Riane Eisler and David Loye, *The Partnership Way: New Tools for Living and Learning* (Brandon, VT: Holistic Education Press, 1998).

Riane Eisler and Alfonso Montuori, "Creativity, Society, and the Hidden Subtext of Gender," in *Social Creativity*, eds., Alfonso Montuori and Ronald Purser (Hampton Press, in press).

Anne Fausto-Sterling, *Myths of Gender* (New York: Basic Books, 1985).

Carol Gilligan, *In a Different Voice* (Cambridge, MA: Harvard University Press, 1982).

Paul Kivel, *Men's Work: How to Stop the Violence That Tears Our Lives Apart* (New York: Ballantine Books, 1992).

Jean Baker Miller, *Toward a New Psychology of Women* (Boston: Beacon Press, 1976).

Ilya Perlingieri, *Sofonisba Anguissola* (New York: Rizzoli, 1992).

Nikolas Platon, *Crete* (Geneva: Nagel Publishers,1966).

Autumn Stanley, *Mothers and Daughters of Invention: Notes for a Revised History of Technology* (Metuchen, NJ: Scarecrow Press, 1993).

Ethlie Ann Vare and Greg Ptaceck, *Mothers of Invention* (New York: William Morrow and Co., 1988).

RIANE EISLER J.D. is best known for her groundbreaking book *The Chalice and the Blade: Our History, Our Future,* which has been hailed by the anthropologist Ashley Montagu as "the most important book since Darwin's *Origin of Species*" and translated into sixteen languages. Eisler's most recent book, *Sacred Pleasure: Sex, Myth and the Politics of the Body,* is also receiving wide use and critical praise, as have her earlier books, *The Partnership Way, Dissolution,* and *The Equal Rights Handbook.* Her forthcoming book, *Tomorrow's Children: Partnership Education for the 21st Century,* proposes a new primary and secondary school curriculum that can equip young people to meet the challenges they face.

Dr. Eisler is president of the Center for Partnership Studies in Pacific Grove, California, founder of the Alliance for a Caring Economy, and a consultant to business and government on the partnership model as the organization for the 21st century. She is internationally known as a cultural historian, system and evolutionary theorist, educational consultant, and charismatic speaker. She is a fellow of the World Academy of Art and Science and of the World Business Academy.

Chapter 5

The Spiritual Practice

Art although produced by man's hands, is something not created by hands alone, but something which wells up from a deeper source out of our soul. . . . My sympathies in the literary as well as in the artistic field are drawn most strongly to those artists in whom I see most the working of the soul.

— Vincent Van Gogh

Intention and Creativity: Art as Spiritual Practice

PAT B. ALLEN, PH.D., A.T.R.

We are all constantly creating. We create thoughts, feelings, and ideas that construct our view of the world and our experience of reality. It seems funny to me when people come to the Open Studio Project and say, "I want to see if I am creative." They are close to the truth. When we make art we see that we create, but also what we create. Making visual art is a way of becoming acquainted with our thoughts, feelings, and ideas. We become aware of the stories we are living. When these are visible to us, we can choose whether or not they serve us, whether or not we are creating the world we truly want. Coming to know mind and achieve awareness of what mind is creating is a goal of spiritual practice. When we engage in art and writing toward this end, we open ourselves not only to what mind is presently creating — often a frenetic monkey-chase of judgments, guilts, and circular thoughts — but to what mind *can* create — beauty, wisdom, meaning.

The arts are especially wonderful means for exploring creativity because they afford so many pleasures: color, shape, sound. The pleasure of creativity is important because look-ing at mind can be a challenge. We see our judgments, self-criticisms, feelings of worthlessness, and jealousies, and often it is the sheer pleasure of, say, blending colors that gives us the motivation and courage to continue.

Intention is crucial in order to experience creativity as a spiritual practice. I began to paint and draw in college and quickly encountered the common roadblocks of inner voices saying "This isn't real work," "How will you support yourself?" "You couldn't possibly be an artist." It was also true that I had a strong desire to help others, and making art, as it was taught in those days, seemed quite self-indulgent. Then I discovered the field of art therapy and felt I'd hit the jackpot: a way to help through art.

An art therapist helps others engage in their creativity as a way to help their healing and self-understanding. I began by engaging in my own art making. With the help of a teacher, I tried to plumb my depths by making spontaneous art and try-ing to draw insights from the images. The images, though provocative, were strangely mute. The creative force seems to be best engaged with respect, inviting meaning to reveal itself rather than trying therapeutically to extract meaning.

I began to understand the relationship of intention and cre-ativity in my work as an art therapist. Over time, however, I lost my own art. My intention had been to help others; I didn't real-ize how that intention left me out. When this awareness dawned, for a while I returned my focus to my art and let go of helping others. Eventually, I came to realize that making art is my spiritual practice, and my adherence to it is necessary nourishment if I am to be of service to the world. Rather than some kind of self-indulgence, making art is life sustaining. Through art making I make way for the creative force to manifest. I also learned that our culture's emphasis on the solitary artist, the mad genius alone in a room, is a debilitating image. Working alongside others, gaining support and witness from others, is a crucial aspect of the creative process. Nothing in the natural world exists in isolation; all forms of life exist as an interconnected, interdependent web. I looked for like-minded others, and together we crafted a simple intention: to make art and be of service to the world. Our intention manifested as the Open Studio Project, a place for us to invite others to engage in art and writing and come to know themselves, one another, and the world.

Through my training in art therapy I learned that it was my job to direct this process for others, and so I used images toward a certain end. "Draw your pain" or "draw your family" are directives I gave to others as I tried to understand their experiences. My intention was to help, to gain information that would enhance our understanding of the client's suffering. My intention was to be a good therapist and to help others.

Rabbi David Cooper, in his book *God Is a Verb*, reminds us:

> It is important for us to understand that an intention behind an act does not ensure its results. Intention must be balanced by awareness. The greater the awareness, the greater the probability that something good will come out. The denser the awareness, even though one's intentions may be good, the greater the risk that

things will not turn out so well. We could do something kindhearted for someone without realizing that this could bring enormous grief into his or her life.*

The therapeutic paradigm is a product of rather dense awareness, recognizing extremes of psychic pain, but often failing to see the resources for healing inherent in each individual's symptoms. Creativity is inclusive and nonjudgmental. Our symptoms are visitors in our stories and are welcomed. We invite them to speak and share their wisdom.

My art making has proved to be a wonderful means to refine my awareness. Over time, through working extensively with my images, I began to learn that the creative force has its own intention. I was experimenting with a technique called a scribble drawing: after doing a series of stretching exercises, I drew a loose series of lines as a starting point for an image. My only intention was to see what would emerge. One day the head of a dark woman appeared in the scribble. She was clad in an elaborate headdress, her face veiled. Rich pinks and purples and elaborate jewels adorned her covering, including mirrored pieces that reflected my face. She directed each stroke I made on the paper. My thinking mind immediately became enchanted with her, naming her as a manifestation of the Divine feminine, something I was longing to understand. My artistic ego wanted to turn a line above her head into a snake, surely a worthy attribute of the Goddess. The paper suddenly refused to accept the green chalk pastel I was using. I sat, confused, until I heard or felt the image suggest turning that line

---

* *God Is a Verb* (Riverhead Books, 1997), p. 141.

into a rose. It was as if I had insulted a guest by naming her before she introduced herself. She gently corrected me by allowing the rose to be drawn while refusing the snake.

The image has a life of her own and a lesson to teach me. The lesson of the rose is different from the lesson of the snake, and I may not know which is right for me at a particular moment. I came to believe that I have no idea what another person should be drawing, let alone doing, that my purpose is indeed not to direct the art making of others toward some kind of therapeutic outcome, but rather to create an environment in which others can discover their images and be directed by them. I began to understand that creativity isn't merely a human attribute, but rather that creativity is a facet of the Divine intelligence of the universe. To create means to walk on holy ground, to engage with the Divine, and to experience it moving through me to manifestation. This force, by whatever name we call it, is constantly offering to show us how things work. We are called to resonate with a force greater than ourselves, yet we each remain a unique note in the overall song of creation. To be in service to one's creativity is a form of spiritual practice. It requires an open heart, an accepting body, a quiet mind.

As my awareness of this reality grows, I see that there is ultimately only one intention: I surrender to the Divine, the creative life force, and welcome its manifestation through me. Now this is not possible if I am trying to manage or direct this force, if I am trying to meet the needs of my ego by way of creative work. The ego can direct some energetic making and doing that can dazzle the eye, enchant the viewer, and draw attention my way. But the ego requires someone else to be inferior if I am to be valued. The ego requires judgments and the projection of authority onto a teacher, juror, or gallery owner. As we create in relationship to the Divine, we come to know our intrinsic value, our preciousness, our uniqueness, and our interconnectedness. We know this not because we see and judge another as inferior, as a better or worse artist. We are aware of our wholeness as well as the wholeness of others, which include intrinsic power and authority. The need for validation from some outside source begins to seem silly. We seek to share with others because our beauty is reflected in theirs and theirs in ours; creativity becomes a wonderful dance and not a contest with a scarcity of prizes.

The greatest paradox of creative engagement with the Divine is that I as creator fall away. Instead, in viewing my work, the viewer forgets that someone made it and instead awakens to her longing for engagement with creativity. When I wrote *Art is a Way of Knowing*, every time I sat down to write I prayed to be an instrument of the Divine, to have the words come through me that were needed in the world. Although all the art and experiences contained in the book are certainly from my life, when reading it I have the interesting experience of thinking, "Who wrote this?" When people tell me, apologetically, that they got only halfway through the book and never finished because they began making their own art, I am humbly delighted.

The scribble drawings were my beginning of art making as a spiritual practice. My intention was no longer to draw a tree, but to practice openness to whatever came. Opening to the creative force means allowing the river of life force energy to flow through me. The energy flows through me most completely when I am aligned in body, mind, and heart. Yet, in another wonderful paradox, making images serves to bring about this very alignment. When I am working and feel my energy wane or suddenly disappear, I know that something is out of alignment. Perhaps an inner censor has arisen to judge an image as too raw, too sweet, somehow not worthy of expression. I may be resisting an insight about my life the image is presenting to me. I may be ignoring a physical need such as the need to rest, or exercise, or eat. I have come to trust the creative force so completely that I have faith that whatever truth is needed in any moment will be revealed if only I stop and pay attention. There is nothing singular about me. The Divine requires each of us in order to manifest her infinite being. We are each a celebration of Divine life force energy, unique yet interconnected, each precious. We each have the choice to say Yes! in any moment.

Ultimately, the creative force will not be denied. If we shut her out, she will knock more forcefully on our door, she will come in disturbing dreams to awaken us to our true nature. If we block all other access, our bodies will create illness or injury to get our attention. If we can imagine for a moment that our every experience is an opportunity for us to engage with the Divine, to meet her and receive her unending gifts, our lives can become holy, whole. If we choose to meet her consciously, intentionally, we enter the realm of the beloved. We are showered with gifts beyond our wildest imagining. All that is needed is the intention to open to the creative force. We do this by writing an intention in simple language. If you wish to engage in art making, your intention could be something like, "I have the time and opportunity to paint." If you have the opportunity but can't allow yourself to get into it, try, "I enjoy expressing myself through art." An all-purpose one is "I open to the creative force," but pay attention, the universe may manifest in unexpected ways.

The lessons are many and subtle. There is enormous pleasure in using art materials, yet we also learn simple lessons about care and concern as we wash our paint brushes to ensure they will serve us in the creation of the next image. Our intention begins to extend into our lives when we begin to care on more subtle levels about our bodies, our possessions, our homes, not in the sense of grasping or possessiveness, but in the sense of honoring our bodies and having gratitude for the things that support our lives. Our senses are enlivened as we apply paint to paper; our eyes are clearer when we leave the studio and return to the world. We are less numb to the dishevelment of our environment when we see it with clear eyes, more likely to take care how we treat the earth and one another. In the studio I create alongside others and am constantly shown the beauty and uniqueness of each person, so I realize that each being is precious. I grow in empathy as I watch the creative force manifest through others. Soon, I see others even outside the studio as conduits of the Divine. When we do this on a regular basis, we are created anew. These are daily truths that unfold over and over. Our awareness is continually refined. It is not so much that we create images that belong in museums, to be held in some sort of awe, but that we experience continuous revelations about life, ourselves, our relationships with others. We recognize that the river of life force energy flows in each of us, that we can dip our cup into it at any moment and be nourished, that it is not the province of the few but the birthright of all. The intention of the Divine is for us to know and enjoy this simple truth.

※

PAT B. ALLEN, PH.D., A.T.R., is an artist and writer with more than twenty years experience as an art therapist. She is cofounder and codirector of the Open Studio Project, Inc., a community arts studio in Chicago dedicated to art making as a form of spiritual practice for personal and social transformation. She teaches at the School of the Art Institute of Chicago and for eight years was on the faculty of the University of Illinois. She has lectured and presented workshops throughout the United States. Her artwork has been exhibited widely. She is the author of *Art Is a Way of Knowing: A Guide to Self-Knowledge and Spiritual Fulfillment Through Creativity* (Shambhala, 1995) as well as many articles in the field of art therapy. The Open Studio Project welcomes inquiries and visits and is located at 1739 N. Damen Avenue, Chicago, IL 60647, (773) 772-2172.

Brush with God — Creativity as Practice and Prayer

ADRIANA DÍAZ

*I*t's fascinating to reflect on one's childhood and the early undisciplined brushstrokes that created the eventual mural of one's life. In my first thirty years spirituality and art developed in separate corners, so distant that I never imagined they would one day meet in the center. There were times when I felt abandoned by God and focused all my attention on art. At other times, despairing of art I turned to God for perseverance and strength.

There were, of course, moments of exhilaration, when the two merged and lifted me like a pair of giant wings: listening to the mysterious strains of Saint Saëns wafting through the rose-windowed vaultings of Notre Dame de Paris, lingering in the haunting shadows of Granada's Alhambra, and gazing at Monet's paintings of Rouen Cathedral for the first time. For most of my early life, however, prayer and painting were two separate practices — one sacred, the other profane. The creative practice I now enjoy is the culmination of an integrative process that took long determination and discipline. The rewards are so valuable to me and to the students whose lives I've subsequently touched that I'm grateful for every step.

The spiritual corner of my early mural was ruled by black-and-white-habited Dominican sisters marching my innocent little mind in and out of Roman Catholic catechism. Each Saturday afternoon I went to confession, Sunday mornings, to mass and Holy Communion. I loved the interior space of the church, the hollow sounds of the kneelers unfolding, the scent and shimmering shadows of candles. I loved the starched white linens on the altars, the polished gold chalice, the colorful robes, and especially the bells. The Lenten season meant a weekly practice of Stations of the Cross and the sacred stench of frankincense. Each May I built an altar in my room for the celebration of the Blessed Virgin. I was a chatty, pious little girl, diligent about her studies and genuinely determined to win sainthood through a personal encounter with the Holy Mother.

The creativity corner of my life was a deeply private place dominated by a box of enchanted crayons. It wasn't actually the crayons themselves that held the power; it was the colors. Lifting the lid of their green-and-gold box, I entered a world of living playmates. Each color had a personality. The colors had arguments, love affairs, and friendship problems. I was the confidante and mediator they were always happy to see. We would talk over their problems as we did the day's work together. I put them on everything: paper dolls, coloring books, old note pads, once even on the living room carpet. I was an only child, and they were my friends.

My mother, who was happiest when I was home under her

custodial surveillance, escalated my interest in art with a set of paint-by-number pictures. Immediately I fell in love with the smell of paint and linseed oil, and although I never would have admitted it then, moving those colors around with that little brush was the most heavenly experience I'd known. Even though I was sure it wouldn't get me a visit from the Virgin Mary, I knew I loved painting more than prayer.

My favorite part of paint-by-numbers came when the puzzle paintings were finished and small amounts of paint were left in the little containers. No numbers, no lines, no guidance. With joyful trepidation I became mesmerized by the feel and process of painting while naively creating every visual cliché known to the working class: farmhouses by a river, barefoot boys fishing from a wooden bridge, and stiff ballerinas standing on pointe.

Sadly, however, the deeper I went into religion and the higher I went in art education, the more distanced I became from the powerful and hypnotic experiences of my youth. After having had such a hopeful foundation for a creative and spiritually rich life, at twenty-two I felt religiously orphaned and confused about the meaning of art. More than that, I doubted my ability to successfully engage in either. I had been taught a practice of religious conventions rather than guided toward an intimate relationship with God. I had been trained in the craft of art, but taught nothing about how to connect that craft to the expression of my soul.

Neither church teachers nor art professors addressed the "I," that "I" longing to make its unique connection and contribution to God and Art. It took years for me to realize that my studies had been for the sake of training; putting heart and soul into the text of my work was the dimension of art one eventually confronts alone. Now I had to go beyond being a trained person: I had to become an art-ist, one whose soul is expressed through the skills of one's craft.

I continued to study art beyond my undergraduate degree, pursuing also studies in psychology, literature, religion, and anthropology until I eventually earned a masters' degree in culture and spirituality. Through those years of study I finally learned that the power of a person's work is rooted as much in personal character as it is in skills honed for that work. In her enduring book, *If You Want to Write*, Brenda Ueland referred to this as "the Third Dimension" — the nature, character, and personality of the artist evident in any work.

While high character is no prerequisite for art, there is a unique kind of integrity that art demands. Some great artists have been liars and cheats, philanderers and thieves, alcoholics, maniacs, and depressives. But when they made their art it was all there, every inch of weakness and strength, every iota of goodness and evil. Everything was given up as a gift to the gods without one inch of shadow withheld. Through every celebration of the creative process, the artist puts his or her Self on the altar, fully present. And that kind of integrity — the communion of action and identity — is the cornerstone of both art and worship.

The creative act is a courageous, ancient gesture, a dynamic, prayerful exploration of the dark mystery that is human existence. When I finally identified this face of creativity as sacred practice, I built a small altar in my studio and my work took on a depth of meaning it never had. Prayer and art suddenly meshed and became redefined. Prayer was no longer just a means of saying please and thank you. It wasn't done in pursuit of holiness as I'd been taught back in the child's corner of my life. Prayer became synonymous with art as an authentic expression of my entire complex Self.

Along with my professional work as an artist, I teach painting and writing to adults through a process I call Creative Meditation. Adult students come timidly to my class feeling isolated and ashamed of their private wounds, fearing mostly the possible devastation of continued failure. In their early conversations they realize they share a common language full of "can'ts" and "nevers." This builds the first tool toward healing: community.

Some students are so over trained that their creative expression is paralyzed. Others stopped expressing themselves in childhood because of traumatic experiences. No matter the nature of their past, the most empowering characteristic in those students is their desire to be creatively free. When desire exceeds fear, we can succeed at anything.

We begin our work with the body, the constantly creative biogift in which we were born. The body is an organically creative creature and does not ask permission from the ego to do its work. It grows hair and nails; it transforms oxygen into carbon dioxide; it regenerates skin. It dreams. The innate generative nature of the body is indisputable and leads us to the recognition that the loss of creative expression is a painful affliction of self-alienation.

After we realize the gifts of the body, the mind and spirit quickly blossom as available sources of expressive material. Breathing meditation and visualization are constant tools for the challenging task of freeing the ego, that narcissistic perfectionist usually most concerned with looking good and getting stroked.

Although we need to keep the ego's decision-making and evaluative powers of perception, we also need to relax its insecurities, which can be barriers to fulfillment. The idea of Creative Meditation is to sink into the physical and spiritual experience of the creative process. So we enter creativity as a form of sacred play, focusing on the improvisational adventure of following our materials and trusting that a dynamic series of expressive gestures will happen through us.

Paint, for example, applied onto a wet surface will move according to its nature and its relationship with water. That interaction leads us to respond in a certain way. Learning when to relinquish control to the materials is as important as developing the skills to enhance the materials. This interaction, then, between the Self and the materials calls on us to become aware that our bodies can respond spontaneously, guided by intuition and a certain ancient wisdom that Jung may have attributed to the collective unconscious. That wisdom is a genetic and psychological inheritance from the ancestors. When we think, for example, of the exquisite paintings in the ancient caves of Lascaux and Altamira, we realize that the human is an innately creative animal. Art is an integral part of our evolutionary being.

Life is an amazing, suspenseful phenomenon in which we are both the master and the work. Our joys, sorrows, defeats, and accomplishments ultimately hinge on our ability to relate to mystery. At times we must have the courage to yield control. At other times life demands that we take action, whether we want to or not and whether we know what action to take or not. When Picasso learned from the study of African masks that art was the mediator between human terrors and the unknown forces of the universe, he recognized, as we all must, that creativity is our innate and sacred gift, the ultimate prayer.

We live in a time when technology has taken center stage as a brilliant new human accomplishment. Technology, like paint, clay, or wood, is a medium of expression. Although it has many shiny whistles and bells to captivate the always-curious human mind, we must not mistake technology for culture. Culture grows from the practice of living. The culture of the new millennium will not be created by technology, but by the people who carry that technology into the future. If we are to be cultural collaborators, we must make a daily choice to live expressive lives. We can decide to make the age of technological creativity a new era in the spiritually creative expression of our species.

✴

ADRIANA DÍAZ is a teacher, painter, and author who has used her Creative Meditation methods to change lives, heal psyches, and enrich relationships around the world. She uses creativity as a source of meditation, reflection, ritual, and healing. She is the author of *Freeing the Creative Spirit* (HarperSanFrancisco, 1992).

Becoming Fully Brilliant

JUDITH CORNELL

*M*ore than 2,000 years ago Christ said, "Is it not written in your scriptures that ye are gods?" As souls made in the image of God we have within us the same creative powers as our creator, although most people find that difficult to believe. At one time I, too, did not embrace this truth. Now, it is my hope that in sharing my spiritual journey with you, you will feel inspired to reclaim your divine Self and develop your creative powers from a place of love and wisdom.

The future of our world depends on how we live and create the present moment. To thrive in the new millennium, we must change outmoded thinking and grasp the potent creative nature of our souls. We must remember who we *really* are and take responsibility for our creative actions.

The last hundred years have been described as the "atomic age" or "age of light." When the atomic bomb was used destructively, Albert Einstein said, "We shall require a substantially new manner of thinking if mankind is to survive." In this short time span our potent, creative godlike nature has manipulated electromagnetic energies to create bombs; has restructured DNA to create whole new species; and has created radio, movies, TV, computers, the Internet, lasers for surgery, and on and on.

In the late 1960s while I was studying for my master of fine arts degree in the ceramic arts, my professor of art history asked the class to write a paper on "What Is Art?" During one of his lectures he told us with some disdain that only painters and sculptors could be called artists or true creators. In his mind ceramic arts was a subcategory of crafts. (Today, digital or computer artists are placed in the same subcategory.) What Is Art? I thought dutifully and then wrote about my observations: that we are all creative whether we are painting, sculpting, creating businesses, creating gourmet meals, building rocket ships, or inventing new gadgets. To my perception there seemed almost limitless creative possibilities open to human ingenuity.

I challenged my professor's narrow definition of creativity by saying that the definition of art and creativity needed to expand beyond its present narrow confines to one that includes all human beings. This inclusiveness would acknowledge all our soul gifts to creatively shape our lives and circumstances in our chosen fields. Creativity, in its currently accepted definition, had been viewed as the prerogative of a few rather than as a divine gift within all souls.

People fearfully back away from developing their creative powers because they associate creativity with egocentricity, eccentricity, instability, and even insanity. To awaken the luster of our souls' genius potential, to stay on the cutting edge, and to ensure a better future for our planet, people in all fields — including business, science, and art — need a substantially new manner of thinking about developing creative potential.

When I was in graduate school, art in its secular definition was restricted to objects of painting and sculpture that reflected images either of the outer world or of the psychological or intellectual states of the creator. A hierarchy was created among the galleries of what was acceptable material for "art." Once again I challenged this confining definition to include any material in the universe as suitable for expression. When I wrote that paper, I was not aware scientists had discovered that the only material of the physical universe is energy and that atomic energy is responsible for all the forms we see even though they appear as different objects to our physical eyes. Today, all advanced technology is based on this discovery.

When I read my paper in class more than 30 years ago, the professor stormed out of the classroom, angry and indignant that I had tampered with established definitions. In his wake he left twenty frightened graduate students. I stood there with my mouth open, unable to comprehend why my professor was so upset with my broader perspective. I knew, however, that I had pointed out some profound truth. For many lonely years I held those concepts in my heart and believed that major change needed to happen in the world of art.

For fifteen years I tried to follow the rules of success outlined by the art world. I produced a lot of work, showed in galleries across the United States, and networked at art openings.

I was increasingly unfulfilled as I experienced the deeply competitive cutthroat nature of the business. Many artists I knew experienced deep depression, were doing drugs, or were alcoholics — not a very healthy lifestyle. For these reasons I deeply questioned the purpose of creativity and art.

In 1979 I was ready to stop my artistic endeavors when I had a mystical experience. I experienced the universe as alive and filled with energy. For the first time I felt the presence of God's love permeating the whole universe, including my whole being. In that loving mystical state, God revealed that the noble purpose of art was twofold: Art existed to show the divine unity and oneness of the universe, and it was created to reflect spiritual realities and healing. This purpose was not taught in graduate school nor was it found in any Western books on art. If this indeed was the noble purpose of art, then my consciousness and my art needed to change. I decided that instead of giving up my art I would create images filled with the healing power of God's love while reflecting the unity of the universe.

In 1979 I began my pioneering work to portray these universal concepts. Little did I know that my life was about to change dramatically. My inquiry began with the following question: What is the underlying essence of all reality? "Light," my intuitive voice answered. As soon as the answer came, I experienced a profound, spontaneous, spiritual awakening that totally changed my life and artistic direction. This experience gave me an even deeper understanding of the creative nature of the soul. I also gained greater insight into the sacred purpose of the arts: to reflect states of enlightenment. I learned that by using the creative process of imaginative thought, willpower, and sacred sounds we can create anything and can direct subtle energies within the body to foster healing in mind, body, and spirit.

My awakening began with an explosion of light within my physical body and mind so bright that every element of everyday reality vanished. My sense of people and material objects as separate from myself became, instead, a perception of oneness. I saw the universe and everything in it as a sacred, transparent unity of light and divine intelligence. For me there was no separation between spiritual light or divine intelligence (consciousness) and physical light, except that matter — or atomic structure — appeared more dense in my inner vision.

Within that transparency of light, I observed stages of human evolution. Past, present, and future disappeared, and I was able to see everything happening at once on various levels of consciousness. I felt a sense of an unfolding divine human ability to cocreate the phenomenal world by using and directing light, both inwardly and outwardly. Each stage of human evolution flashed before me as an upward spiral of spiritual development into divine realization.

I saw luminous human figures without form — a transparency of light some have called astral or energy bodies. I saw human beings transformed into more refined transparent bodies of light, gifted with divine power to structure atomic energies into any imaginable form. (In the field of DNA research, for example, we are already capable of doing this.) In this spiritual encounter I had an instantaneous understanding of quantum physics even though I had never studied it. This understanding produced a quantum leap in consciousness and transformed my understanding of art as a separate discipline into one that was integrally connected with science and ancient wisdom. I came to greater intuitive understanding of the nature of atomic energies, which consciousness creatively directs and continually restructures into diverse molecular configurations.

So shocking and all-encompassing was this vision that my sense of duality — good-evil, male-female, light-dark, body-mind — fused into oneness with all creation and the creator. In short, I saw humans becoming refined radiant beings of intelligent light — gods in the making. For me it was like coming out of Plato's cave of darkness into such brilliant light of understanding that my whole being felt as if it had been electrocuted with a new perception of reality.

After this experience I was led to three books: *The Biological Basis of Religion and Genius*, by Gopi Krishna; *Kundalini: Transcendence or Psychosis?,* by Lee Sannella, M.D.; and *Autobiography of a Yogi*, by Paramahansa Yogananda. These references confirmed that I was not crazy, but had had a genuine transcendental experience. I learned from these sources and from my ongoing practice of meditative yoga that awakening to the soul's nature or the true Self takes tremendous creative energy within the human body. This awakening changes not only our consciousness but the very atoms of the body itself. In Eastern literature I found the deep roots of sacred art. I learned of Hindu sages that turned every aspect of human culture — art, science, drama, music, medicine, astronomy, and language

— into tools of spiritual awakening and realization. It has taken me many years to fully integrate the resulting shift in consciousness.

I synthesized inner revelations and my practice of meditative yoga with the roots of sacred art, Western science, and experimentation within various educational settings. I developed an approach to art and consciousness that provides an empirical, experiential way to awaken our souls' creative powers from an inspired level. The model combines the sacred art and spiritual science of the mandala, theories in modern physics, brain research, transpersonal psychology, and cross-cultural spiritual philosophies.

It is by using and developing our creative soul gifts that we can be fully empowered to jointly create a more wholesome world. For this to become a new way of being, we need to awaken from the nightmare of seeing ourselves as limited beings. The more we hold to a diminished image of humanity, the more we become swallowed by low self-esteem, hopelessness, and fear. When we believe ourselves to be without talent or power, we lack the energy we need to bring in new visions of wholeness and of connection with all life. Instead, we act as victims and accept the dictates of a few who feed us images of destruction and project to us a sense of hopelessness.

All is not lost. Embedded within our souls and DNA are the creative possibilities of our enlightenment and future. Our communities, art, music, scientific technologies, and businesses can become life-affirming, harmonious, beautiful, and healing institutions if we are willing to awaken to inspired states of creativity. These soul gifts are the means through which we manifest our individual sparks of divine light. By practicing these gifts with wisdom, love, and compassion, we can contribute to a spiritual renaissance: one in which our creativity reflects the true light of divinity. This renaissance can remake our world.

✷

JUDITH CORNELL, PH.D., is an adjunct professor in the department of East/West Psychology at the California Institute of Intregal Studies. She leads seminars throughout the world integrating art with psychology, philosophy, science, and spirituality. She is founder and director of the organization Manifesting Inner Light. Her books include *AMMACHI: A Biography of One of the Greatest Healers of Our Time* (William Morrow & Co., 2000), *Drawing the Light from Within: Keys to Awaken Your Creative Power* (Quest Books, 1997), and *Mandala: Luminous Symbols for Healing* (Quest Books, 1995), which won the prestigious Benjamin Franklin Award in 1995 for publishing excellence and was named one of the best books of the year by *Body, Mind, Spirit* magazine.

Losing Yourself in the Divine

LUCIA CAPACCHIONE, Ph.D., A.T.R.

*W*hen you create you lose yourself in your creation. Time seems to stand still and all else is forgotten. You participate in the divine play that is creativity. These moments offer a glimpse of who you really are: a being fashioned in the image and likeness of God. Like the source of all creation, you are a creator, too. It is your divine birthright. The person who says "I'm not creative" is uttering blasphemy. The truth is that you are the Creative Self expressing through the human vessel of your body, emotions, mind, and soul. Creativity flows through you as a universal life force, called by many names throughout the ages: *chi, prana,* shakti, the Holy Spirit. It is this energy of love flowing through you that also gives life to your creations.

The medium in which you create is irrelevant. It doesn't matter whether you write a business proposal, play a piano sonata, or prepare a delicious meal. You may be seeking to resolve one of life's mundane problems or to express deep feelings and insights through poetry. Embrace your creation as a lover and you can break through to another realm. When you stick with it for better or for worse, your creation becomes your guru (Sanskrit meaning "from darkness to light").

Losing yourself in the divine embrace of the creative process, you disappear. Your ego or limited sense of separateness vanishes, and you emerge into the vast ocean that is creativity. This is an altered state of intuitive awareness in which you renounce control from your head alone. Instead, you allow the Creative Self to flow through your heart, your body, and your intuition. Then you are taken to places you can never go in your ordinary waking state. This road leads eventually to moments of divine bliss described by ecstatic poets like Rumi, Kabir, and Lalli.

The desire to realize the "natural high" found in peak moments of creativity is so basic that, if given no healthy outlet for this urge, people turn to alcohol or drugs for a simulated version. These counterfeit forms inevitably backfire, for they violate an essential ingredient: the human vessel for containing the Creative Self. And that vessel — physical, emotional, mental, and spiritual — can be shaped only through hard work and awareness. We must harmonize these four aspects of our being. For instance, the body and emotions need time to digest flashes of inspiration the soul and mind receive. After participating in laboratory controlled experiments with LSD many years ago, author Anaïs Nin concluded that she didn't need drugs to get high. Her writing had always taken her to a state of heightened awareness. Nin had kept a journal since childhood, developing her craft every day of her life. Regular writing practice was the cauldron in which Nin, the novelist and essayist, was formed. Interestingly, it is her diaries (published in several volumes) that are best known, even though she hadn't originally intended them for publication.

To flourish, creativity needs our full attention and disciplined focus on details. It is a way of life, a way of being and perceiving. It is a form of meditation that leads out from the Creative Self and back to it. The creative process rests on a foundation of attentiveness, skill, and hard work. At her most inspired, the master pianist loses herself in performance, transcending technique and dissolving into the Creative Self. Her ego steps aside and the music plays her. This is possible only because she has spent years rigorously developing her God-given talent through loving practice. The creative entrepreneur writes an inspired business plan because by acquiring skill, experience, and knowledge he has also cultivated intuition, vision, and love of his work. He's done his homework.

Any practice, spiritual or otherwise, involves making mistakes. Millions of errors are made before the human vehicle is ready for the Creative Self to freely flow through it. A good metaphor is in the art-making process. For instance, in ceramics the clay must be wedged (pounded vigorously to remove air bubbles) before the pot is formed. If not, when the pot is baked in the kiln fire (which is where the transformation occurs), the air pockets will cause the pot to explode. In the creative process we are "wedged" by life, pounded vigorously to remove the air bubbles of an inflated ego.

The yogis call this *tapasya,* the purification in which inner heat is generated by friction between the mind and the heart. The ego dies hard. When the ego is embarrassed by the revelations of our human foibles, omissions, or transgressions, we experience frustration, angry explosions, or the slow inward boil of resentment. In the same way, the creative process is humbling. It opens us to rejection and feelings of failure, self-doubt, and unworthiness. That's why so many people avoid it. Creativity's invisible fire burns up all that stands between us and the integrity of our creation. When we serve the work, however, it becomes our teacher. We shape the work, but at the same time the work shapes us. The alchemists described this purification process as turning base matter into gold, tests into mastery, crisis into wisdom.

In serving the work, truth is everything. For example, what we ignore comes back to haunt us. Weak spots a writer glosses over in a manuscript, baking soda the chef forgets to add to the cake mixture, specifications the designer leaves out of an architectural blueprint become teachers. The pot that cracks apart in the kiln was not wedged properly in the first place. The results never lie.

There's nothing wrong with making mistakes. In fact, mistakes are honorable. They are how we learn. But if we think we're above it all, our egos will be burned in the fire of truth. Through embarrassment we find we didn't know it all. We couldn't slide past the truth. What we missed or chose to ignore inevitably trips us and grounds us again in earthbound reality. Brought back to our senses and to the matter at hand, we are reminded of our human being-ness.

That is the vessel for our divinity. Try to escape that fact and God or the Goddess has no place to reside in us.

If you are devoted to the Creative Self, you will encounter the same tests described in the writings of saints and mystics throughout the ages. These include highs and lows, agonies and ecstasies, inspired moments and dark nights of the soul. Some periods feel charged with "greening" (to use Hildegard of Bingen's term). Juicy and fertile, you are full of "aha" moments — breakthroughs and discoveries. Inspiration gushes like a geyser.

At other times you feel dry, lost in an arid desert of disinterest, depression, and barrenness. Emptiness prevails and you wonder if maybe you haven't lost your talent and skill along with your connectedness to the source of creation. You are haunted with questions like Will I ever have another creative idea? Am I all dried up? Have I used all the creativity rationed to me in this lifetime? A battle with the demons of self-judgment rages within.

The literature of both art and mysticism abounds with descriptions of this phenomenon, a black void that seems totally enveloping and all-pervasive. Read the words of biblical figures like Job, poets like Saint John of the Cross and Rainer Maria Rilke, spiritual leaders like Saint Teresa of Avila, artists like Vincent Van Gogh. They all gave voice to the darkness within where, paradoxically, the Creative Self is to be found. Artist and recovered mental patient Mary Barnes once wrote, "In order to come to the light, I have to germinate in the dark."

You don't have to go out of your way to find these experiences.

We all face our terrors at one time or another. It's part of the human condition — losing a job, filing for divorce, going into bankruptcy, having a serious accident, dealing with a life-threatening illness or the aftermath of a natural disaster, surviving the death of a loved one or the loss of a love. But if you see crisis as an opportunity, an invitation to personal renewal, then life itself becomes a creative process.

Those on the creative path who have journeyed fully into inner darkness and have come back to tell the tale seem to be saying, "These are the dues you have to pay. Life will pound you vigorously. Can you stand up to it? Do you have the strength and tenacity? Do you trust the creative process? Have faith in the source of creation."

Life's tests are the kiln fire that transforms us into conscious vessels of the Creative Self. However, if we cannot embrace challenges as teachers, our human clay can explode. Unable to handle the heat, some cast themselves as victims and become bitter. They may become violent, depressed, take refuge in addictions, resort to criminal behavior, become irretrievably insane, or even commit suicide.

How can the human vessel contain the limitless divine Creative Spirit? Like the birth of a baby, it's a mystery yet it happens every minute. Here the discipline side of the creative process is essential. It has been said that art is five percent inspiration and ninety-five percent perspiration. The same can be said for the creative process of living. You show up each day, do the work (whatever form it takes), follow where your next inspiration leads, and pay attention as the challenges unfold.

This is as true in your occupation as it is in your personal life. When you are committed to seeing your life as a work in progress — as the creative process beckoning to you — then creativity becomes your spiritual practice.

Day after day your devotion to creativity will enable you to merge with your Creative Self. Your destiny will unfold from within. Your life will become the unique work of art it was meant to be. An ancient Chinese story tells of an old master ceramist developing a new glaze for his vases. Each day he carefully regulated the heat in his kiln, worked painstakingly with the chemistry of the glazes, and experimented with them over and over. He labored devotedly day after day, yet the effect he had envisioned continued to elude him. Having applied his vast store of knowledge and skill and having exhausted his human power, the master concluded that his life was over. He climbed into the kiln to be fired along with his vases. When his apprentices opened the kiln, they beheld a magnificent sight. All the glazes were sheer perfection, like nothing their master had ever achieved. He had become one with his creation.

In embracing creativity as our spiritual practice, we commend ourselves into the Creator's hands, knowing that our goal is to disappear. And when we do, we become one with all creation. The divine spirit dances us, it plays its music through us. We become the instrument through which the divine flows like a river to the sea. All the pilgrimages, all the prayers and chants in all the temples and churches of the world are meaningless unless we are devoted to living in and through the Creative Self, to live as the image and likeness of God.

If life force energies are not moving creatively, they will become destructive (as so-called holy wars have taught us). Destructiveness is the Creative Self turned upside down. Something has taken a wrong turn, and, like cancer, it devours the source of its life. The cure is found in creativity.

When your Creative Self calls, go with it. It is God speaking. Listen to your Creative Conscience, the voice of the divine guiding you each day. It resides in your heart. Go there and roam. That is your true temple.

✴

LUCIA CAPACCHIONE, PH.D., A.T.R., is an artist, registered art therapist, and bestselling author of twelve books on applied creativity, healing, and recovery, including *The Creative Journal: The Art of Finding Yourself* (Ohio University Press/Swallow Press, 1979) *Recovery of Your Inner Child* (Simon & Schuster, 1991), *Putting Your Talent to Work* with P. Van Pelt (Health Communications, 1996), and the forthcoming *Visioneering* (Tarcher/Putnam). Her books are used as texts in courses on creativity, psychology, expressive arts therapy, and creative journaling for children and teens. Originator of the Creative Journal Method, Dr. Capacchione has received international acclaim for techniques that unleash creativity through writing and drawing with the nondominant hand. A popular workshop leader and conference speaker, Dr. Capacchione also conducts spiritual retreats, trains health care professionals, and certifies instructors through her Creative Journal Expressive Arts Training Program. As a corporate consultant, she leads creativity seminars, job outplacement programs, and career coaching for major firms, including the Walt Disney Company.

Creating Minds*

DIANE ACKERMAN

*A*ll language is poetry. Each word is a small story, a thicket of meaning. We ignore the picturesque origins of words when we utter them; conversation would grind to a halt if we visualize flamingos whenever someone referred to a *flight* of stairs. But words are powerful mental tolls invented through play. We clarify life's confusing blur with words. We cage flooding emotions with words. We coax elusive memories with words. We educate with words. We don't really know what we think, how we feel, what we ant, or even who we are until we struggle "to find the right words." What do those words consist of? Submerged metaphors, images, actions, personalities, jokes. Seeing themselves reflected in one another's eyes, the Romans coined the word *pupil*, which meant "little doll." *Orchids* take their name from the Greek word for testicles. *Pansy* derives from the French word *pensée*, or thought, because the flower seemed to have such a pensive face. *Bless* originally meant to redden with

* Adapted from *Deep Play*, by permission of Random House, May 1999.

blood, as in sacrifice. Hence "God bless you" literally means "God bathe you in blood."

We inhabit a deeply imagined world that exists alongside the real physical one. Even the crudest utterance, or the simplest, contains the fundamental poetry by which we live. This mind fabric, woven of images and illusions, shields us. In a sense, or rather in all senses, it's a shock absorber. As harsh as life seems to us now, it would feel even worse — hopelessly, irredeemably harsh — if we didn't veil it, order it, relate familiar things, create mental cushions. One of the most surprising facts about us human beings is that we seem to require a poetic version of life. It's not just that some of us enjoy reading or writing poetry, or that many people wax poetic in emotional situations, but that all human beings of all ages in all cultures all over the world automatically tell their story in a poetic way, using the elemental poetry concealed in everyday language to solve problems, communicate desires and needs, even talk to themselves. When people invent new words, they do so playfully, poetically — computers have *viruses,* one can *surf* the Internet, a naive person is *clueless.* In time, people forget the etymology or choose to disregard it. A plumber says he'll use a gasket on a leaky pipe, without considering that the word comes from *garçonette,* the Old French word for a little girl with her hymen intact. We dine at chic restaurants from porcelain dinner plates, without realizing that when smooth, glistening *porcelain* was invented in France long ago, someone with a sense of humor thought it looked as smooth as the vulva of a pig, which is indeed what *porcelain* means. When we stand by our scruples we don't think of our feet, but the word comes from the Latin *scupulus,* a tiny stone that was the smallest unit of weight. Thus a scrupulous person is so sensitive he's irritated by the smallest stone in his shoe. For the most part, we are all unwitting poets.

Just as the world of deep play exists outside of ordinary life, the poetic world of humans exists within — separate from — ordinary reality. So deep play lives at two removes from the real world (whatever that is), except when we play through the art form we call poetry. Then we stare straight at our inherently poetic version of life, make it even more vigorous and resourceful. Poetry speaks to everyone, but it cries out to people in the throes of vertiginous passions, or people grappling with knotty emotions, or people trying to construe the mysteries of existence.

✳

Poetry was all I knew to write at eighteen. Much has happened in my writerly life since then. Although I still write poetry, I've learned to write prose, too, and that has brought its own frustrations and freedoms. In both genres, writing is my form of celebration and prayer, but it's also the way in which I explore the world, sometimes writing about nature, sometimes about human nature. I always try to give myself to whatever I'm writing with as much affectionate curiosity as I can muster, in order to understand a little better what being human is, and what it was like to have once been alive on the planet, how if felt in one's senses, passions, and contemplations. In that sense, I use art as an instrument to unearth shards of truth. Writing is also the avenue that most often leads me to deep play.

These days, I so that more often in prose. But the real source of my creativity continues to be poetry. I've just published a new collection. I love to read books of poetry. My prose often contains what are essentially prose poems. Why does poetry play such an important role in my life? For centuries, poetry was vital to the life of nearly everyone. In the nineteenth century, poets such as Byron and Tennyson were celebrities of Hollywood status. Movies and television may draw more viewers now, but poetry continues to inspire us, reveal is to one another, and teach us important truths about being human.

The reason is simple: poetry reflects the heart and soul of a people. There is nothing like poetry to throw light into the dark corners of existence, and make life's runaway locomotive slow down for a moment so that it can be enjoyed. Science and technology explain much of our world. Psychology tells us more about human behavior; all three succeed by following orderly rules and theories. Poetry offers truths based on intuition, a keen eye, and the tumultuous experiences of the poet.

✳

The best poems are rich with observational truths. Above all, we ask the poet to teach us a way of seeing, lest one spend a lifetime on this planet without noticing how green light sometimes flares up as the setting sun rolls under.

When Cathy and I were cycling the other day, she mentioned that reading poetry frightened her.

"What if I don't get the real meaning?" she asked. "What if I read 'a ghostly galleon' and think it's referring to a ship, when it's really referring to the lost innocence of America?" I was dumbfounded. Someone had taught her, and many other, that poems work like safes — crack the code and the safe opens to reveal its treasure.

"There are many ways to read a poem," I said, "After all, you don't really know what was going through the poet's mind. Suppose he was having a tempestuous affair with a neighbor, and once when they were alone he told her that her hips were like *a ghostly galleon.* He might then have used the image in a poem he was writing because it fit well, but also as a sly flirtation with his neighbor, whose hips would be secretly commemorated in the verse."

"Do poets do that?" she asked, slightly scandalized that noble thoughts might be tinged with the profane.

"I've done it," I admitted with a grin. "I presume other poets do."

I went on to explain, as teachers of the writerly arts do, that poems dance with many veils. Read a poem briskly, and it will speak to you briskly. Delve, and it will give you rich ore to contemplate. Each time you look, a new scintillation may appear, one you missed before.

✺

Whatever artform one chooses, whatever materials and ideas, the creative siege is the same. One always finds rules, always tremendous concentration, entrancement, and exaltation, always the tension of spontaneity caged by restriction, always risk of failure and humiliation, always the drumbeat of rituals, always the willingness to be shaken to the core, always an urgent need to stain the willows with a glance.

The world is drenched with color, and nature is full of spectacles. You would think that would be enough. Yet we are driven to add even more sensations to the world, to make our thoughts and feelings visible through works of art. We create art for many reasons. As a form of praise and celebration. To impose an order on the formless clamor of the world. As a magical intermediary between us and the hostile, unpredictable universe. For religious reasons, in worship. For spiritual reasons, to commune with others. To temporarily stop a world that seems too fast, too random, too chaotic. To help locate ourselves in nature, and give us a sense of home. Art brings pattern, meaning, and perspective to life. We keep trying to sum life up, to frame small parts of it, to break it into eye-gulps, into visual morsels that are easier to digest. The styles of art may differ widely — Dürer's rhinoceros; a Japanese brush painting — but all are concerned with motion, balance, symmetry, color, order, meaning. We also create art as a powerful form of deep play. Even at its most lawless, it has rules, a pattern and logic missing from everyday life, a chance to make believe. It allows each artist to put herself in harmony with the universe, to find a balance, however briefly, in life's hurricane. For me this becomes most personal in poetry, but others relish creative mischief of a different sort.

✳

An imaginative chronicler of the world's splendor, DIANE ACKERMAN is a poet, essayist, naturalist, and explorer. She has taught at Columbia and Cornell universities and writes for such magazines as *National Geographic,* the *New York Times,* and *The New Yorker,* where she is a staff writer. She is author of several books exploring the natural world, including *A Natural History of Love, The Moon by Whale Light, The Rarest of the Rare,* and *A Natural History of the Senses,* which inspired the 1995 PBS series she hosted. Her new book *Deep Play* will be released by Random House in May 1999.

The Power of Art

KENT NERBURN, Ph.D.

ast night was New Year's Eve. There was a concert on television, a rerun of Leonard Bernstein conducting Beethoven's Ninth Symphony in the Berlin Spielhaus on New Year's Eve, 1989.

I remembered reading about it when it happened. It was an extraordinary concert for an extraordinary time. The Berlin Wall had fallen. People in Eastern Europe were alive with a joy we in America can only imagine. The atmosphere was heady, intoxicating, giddy with the thrill of freedom.

Musicians had gathered from the Soviet Union, the United States, and all over Europe for the performance. Choirs had been massed from around the world.

Leonard Bernstein had been asked to conduct. There he stood, a Jew who had lived through the dark years of the Holocaust, in the midst of the city that had symbolized both the Nazi regime and the division of the world into the camps of communism and democracy, preparing to lead an orchestra and chorus from the nations of the world in a song of healing and celebration.

He was also dying.

What a moment. What an affirmation. What a valedictory for a man who had given his life to the joy and power of music.

The faces of the orchestra members, the beaming of the children in the choir, the quiet, intense electricity of those in the audience all spoke of an event beyond our imagining.

All was coming together: the great vision and horror of the Germanic genius, the triumphant victory of the human spirit over the power of politics; Beethoven in his majesty, Schiller's powerful poetry of freedom; the memory of the death camps, the unity of a people too long divided; the old year — the old epoch — giving way to a new as walls crumbled and a great surge of long-suppressed human emotion swept across the globe.

Bernstein raised his baton and it all came pouring forth — the joy, the sadness, the power and the majesty — rising over the ghostly memory of six million dead and the anguish of years of exile for the human spirit.

The instruments sang as if with one voice. The music rose and expanded and became pure emotion.

Tears streamed from my eyes. I wept uncontrollably. It was more than I was, and more than I could ever be. It was a healing and a testament to the best of who we are and the worst of who we are. It was confession, it was celebration. It was us at our most human.

By the time the concert was over, I had been transformed. Into my daily life had come a moment of sheer beauty. Though at an electronic distance, I had been in the presence of one of those moments that only art can provide, when we humans bring forth something from nothing, and invest it with a majesty and beauty that seems to rival the visions of the gods.

This is the power of art, and the person who has not experienced it is only half alive.

It lives in music, it lives in theater, it lives in painting and architecture and sculpture. It can come in the words of a poem or on the pages of a novel.

I can measure my life by the moments when art transformed me — standing in front of Michelangelo's *Duomo Pieta,* listening to Dylan Thomas read his poetry, hearing Bach's cello suites for the first time.

But not only there.

Sitting at a table in a smoky club listening to Muddy Waters and Little Walter talk back and forth to each other through their instruments; listening to a tiny Japanese girl play a violin sonata at a youth symphony concert; standing in a clapboard gift shop on the edge of Hudson Bay staring at a crudely carved Inuit image of a bear turning into a man.

It can happen anywhere, anytime. You do not have to be in some setting hallowed by greatness, or in the presence of an artist honored around the world. Art can work its magic any time you are in the presence of a work created by someone who has gone inside the act of creation to become what they are creating. When this takes place time stands still and if our hearts are open to the experience, our spirits soar and our imaginations fly unfettered.

You need these moments if you are ever to have a life that is more than the sum of the daily moments of humdrum affairs.

If you can create these moments — if you are a painter or

a poet or a musician or an actor — you carry within you a prize of great worth. If you cannot create them, you must learn to love one of the arts in a way that allows the power of another's creation to come alive within you.

Once you love an art enough that you can be taken up in it, you are able to experience an echo of the great creative act that mysteriously has given life to us all.

It may be the closest any of us can get to God.

KENT NERBURN holds a Ph.D. in religion and art and is an internationally recognized sculptor with works in such settings as the Peace Museum in Hiroshima, Japan, and Westminster Benedictine Abbey in Mission, British Columbia. For several years he worked with the Ojibwe of northern Minnesota, helping collect the memories of the tribal elders. He is the author of *Simple Truths, A Haunting Reverence, Letters to My Son, Small Graces,* and the award-winning *Neither Wolf nor Dog* (all published by New World Library).

Copyright Holders

The essays in this book were created for this collection. The following is a list of contributors' copyrights.

Foreword © 1999 Angeles Arrien

Introduction © 1999 Tona Pearce Myers

"Creating Minds" excerpted and adapted from *Deep Play* © 1999 by Diane Ackerman. Reprinted by permission of Random House.

"Intention and Creativity: Art as Spiritual Practice," © 1998 Pat B. Allen

"Writer and Witness — Healing Through Story," © 1998 Christina Baldwin

"Creativity and the Heart of Shamanism," © 1998 Hal Zina Bennett

"The Healing Power of Creativity," © 1998 Echo Bodine

"Creativity: The Alchemy of Aphrodite," © 1998 Jean Shinoda Bolen, M.D.

"Listening: The Key to Deep Creativity," © 1998 Don Campbell

"Losing Yourself in the Divine" © 1998 Lucia Cappacchione

"Inside the Heartbeat of Creation," © 1998 Michelle Cassou

"Becoming Fully Brilliant," © 1998 Judith Cornell

"Brush with God — Creativity as Practice and Prayer," © 1998 Adriana Díaz

"Creativity and Social Healing" © 1998 Riane Eisler

"Uncertainty — Building Creative Behavior," © 1998 Linda A. Firestone, Ph.D.

"Words from the Marrow," © 1998 John Fox

"Become a Creative Force," © 1998 Robert Fritz

"The Creative Soul Lives in the Shadows," © 1998 Aviva Gold

"Hearing the Audience," © 1998 Robert Grudin

"Taming the Lion," © 1998 Jean Liedloff

"Two Dragonflies and a Volcano," © 1998 Ann Linnea

"The Power of Failure," © 1998 Eric Maisel

"The Practice of Creativity in the Workplace," © 1998 Shaun McNiff

"The Natural Artistry of Dreams," excerpted and adapted from *The Natural Artistry of Dreams: Creative Ways to Bring the Wisdom of Dreams to Waking Life* by Jill Mellick © 1996 by Jill Mellick used by permission from Conari Press

"Saving the Cat," © 1998 Stephen Nachmanovitch

"The Power of Art," excerpted from *Letters to My Son* by Kent Nerburn © 1999 by Kent Nerburn used by permission from New World Library

"Creativity — The Healing Journey Inward," © 1998 Jan Phillips

"Make It Real," © 1998 SARK

Permissions Acknowledgments

Grateful acknowledgment is given to the following publishers and copyright holders for permission to reprint in *The Soul of Creativity:*

Diane Ackerman: Excerpted from *Deep Play* by Diane Ackerman © 1999. Reprinted by permission from Random House.

Odysseus Elytis: Excerpted from "With what stones, what blood, and what iron . . ." from Odysseus Elytis: *Selected Poems* by Odysseus Elytis, translated by Edmund Keeley and Philip Sherrard, et. al. Translation copyright © 1981 by Edmund Keeley and Philip Sherrard. Used by permission of Viking Penguin, a division of Penguin Putnam Inc.

Donna Kennedy: Excerpt from "Ritual," © Donna Kennedy. Reprinted by permission of the author.

Marilyn Krysl: Excerpt from "Saying Things," from *More Palamino, Please, More Fuchsia* by Marilyn Krysl © Marilyn Krysl. Reprinted by permission of The Cleveland State University Poetry Center.

Phillip Levine: Excerpted from "Silent in America," from *Not This Pig* © 1968 by Phillip Levine, Wesleyan University Press, by permission of University Press of New England.

Peter Levitt: Excerpt "Already at birth I was parted . . ." from *One Hundred Butterflies* by Peter Levitt © Peter Levitt. Reprinted by permission of the author.

Barbara McEnerney: Excerpts from "Underneath" and "What Holds," © Barbara McEnerney. Reprinted by permission of the author.

Jill Mellick: Excerpted and adapted from *The Natural Artistry of Dreams: Creative Ways to Bring the Wisdom of Dreams to*

Waking Life by Jill Mellick © 1996 by Jill Mellick used by permission from Conari Press.

Kimberley Nelson: Excerpted from "No Place for Solitude," © Kimberley Nelson. Reprinted by permission of the author.

Kent Nerburn: Excerpted from *Letters to My Son* by Kent Nerburn © 1999 by Kent Nerburn used by permission from New World Library.

William Stafford: Except from "A Ritual to Read to Each Other," © 1960, 1998 by the Estate of William Stafford. Reprinted from *The Way It Is: New & Selected Poems* by William Stafford with the permission of Graywolf Press, Saint Paul, Minnesota.

Ruth Stone: Except from "Advice," © Ruth Stone. Reprinted by permission of the author.

Every effort has been made to contact all rights holders of the material in *The Soul of Creativity*. The editor promises to correct any omissions or mistakes in acknowledgments in future editions.

Recommended Reading

Ackerman, Diane. *Deep Play.* New York: Random House, Inc., 1999.

Allen, Pat B. *Art Is a Way of Knowing: A Guide to Self-Knowledge and Spiritual Fulfillment Through Creativity.* Boston: Shambhala Publications, 1995.

Baldwin, Christina. *Life's Companion: Journal Writing as a Spiritual Quest.* New York: Bantam Doubleday Dell, 1990.

Bennett, Hal Zina. *Write from the Heart: Unleashing the Power of Your Creativity.* Novato, CA: Nataraj/New World Library, 1995.

Bodine, Echo. *Passion to Heal: The Ultimate Guide to Your Healing Journey.* Novato, CA: New World Library, 1993.

Bolen, Jean Shinoda. *Goddesses in Everywoman: A New Psychology of Women.* New York: HarperCollins, 1985.

Cameron, Julia. *The Artist's Way: A Spiritual Path to Higher Creativity.* New York: J. P. Tarcher, 1992.

——— *The Artist's Way at Work: Riding the Dragon: Twelve Weeks to Creative Freedom.* New York: William Morrow & Co., 1998.

Campbell, Don. *The Mozart Effect: Tapping the Power of Music to Heal the Body, Strengthen the Mind, and Unlock the Creative Spirit.* New York: Avon Books, 1997.

Capacchione, Lucia. *The Creative Journal: The Art of Finding Yourself.* North Hollywood, CA: Newcastle Publishing Co., 1989.

——— *The Power of Your Other Hand.* North Hollywood, CA: Newcastle Publishing Co., 1988.

Cassou, Michelle. *Life, Paint and Passion: Reclaiming the Magic of Spontaneous Expression.* New York: J. P. Tarcher, 1996.

Cornell, Judith. *Drawing the Light from Within: Keys to Awaken Your Creative Power.* Wheaton, IL: Quest Books, 1997.

Díaz, Adriana. *Freeing the Creative Spirit: Drawing on the Power of Art to Tap the Magic and Wisdom Within.* San Francisco: HarperSanFrancisco, 1992.

Eisler, Riane. *The Chalice and the Blade: Our History, Our Future.* San Francisco: Harper & Row, 1988.

———— *Sacred Pleasure: Sex, Myth, and the Politics of the Body.* San Francisco: HarperSanFrancisco, 1996.

Firestone, Linda A. *Awakening Minerva: The Power of Creativity in Women's Lives.* New York: Warner Books, 1997.

Fox, John. *Finding What You Didn't Lose: Expressing Your Truth and Creativity Through Poem-Making.* New York: Jeremy P. Tarcher/G.P. Putnam Son's, 1995.

———— *Poetic Medicine: The Healing Art of Poem-Making.* New York: Jeremy P. Tarcher/G.P. Putnam Son's, 1997.

Fritz, Robert. *Creating: A Guide to the Creative Process.* New York: Fawcett Columbine, 1993.

Goleman, Daniel, Paul Kaufman, Michael Ray. *The Creative Spirit.* New York: Plume, 1993.

Gold, Aviva. *Painting from the Source: Awakening the Artist's Soul in Everyone.* New York: HarperCollins, 1998.

Goldberg, Natalie. *Living Color: A Writer Paints Her World.* New York: Bantam Books, 1997.

———— *Writing Down the Bones: Freeing the Writer Within.* Boston: Shambalha Publications, 1998.

Gray, Dorothy Randall. *Soul Between the Lines: Freeing Your Creative Spirit Through Writing.* New York: Avon Books, 1998.

Grudin, Robert. *Time and the Art of Living.* New York: Houghton Mifflin Co., 1998.

Halifax, Joan. *The Fruitful Darkness: Reconnecting with the Body of the Earth.* San Francisco: HarperSanFrancisco, 1994.

Lamott, Anne. *Bird by Bird: Some Instructions on Writing and Life.* New York: Doubleday Books, 1994.

Lee, John. *Writing from the Body: For Writers, Artists, and Dreamers Who Long to Free Your Voice.* New York: St. Martin's Press, 1994.

LeGuin, Ursala. *Steering the Craft: Exercises and Discussions on Story Writing for the Lone Navigator or the Mutinous Crew.* Portland, OR: The Eighth Mountain Press, 1998.

Liedloff, Jean. *The Continuum Concept: In Search of Happiness Lost.* Portland, OR: Perseus Press, 1986.

Linnea, Ann. *Deep Water Passage: A Spiritual Journey at Midlife.* New York: Pocket Books, 1997.

Maisel, Eric. *Fearless Creating: A Step-by-Step Guide to Starting and Completing Your Work of Art.* New York: J. P. Tarcher, 1995.

McNiff, Shaun. *Art as Medicine: Creating a Therapy of the Imagination.* Boston: Shambhala Publications, 1992.

——— *Trust the Process: An Artist's Guide to Letting Go.* Boston: Shambhala Publications, 1998.

Mellick, Jill. *The Natural Artistry of Dreams: Creative Ways to Bring the Wisdom of Dreams to Waking Life.* Berkeley, CA: Conari Press, 1996.

Nachmanovitch, Stephen. *Free Play: Improvisation in Life and Art.* New York: G. P. Putnam & Sons, 1990.

Nerburn, Kent. *Letters to My Son: A Father's Wisdom on Manhood, Life, and Love.* Novato, CA: New World Library, 1999.

Phillips, Jan. *Marry Your Muse: Making a Lasting Commitment to Your Creativity*. Wheaton, IL: Quest Books, 1997.

SARK. *The Bodacious Book of Succulence: Daring to Live Your Succulent Wild Life*. New York: Firestone/Simon & Schuster, 1998.

———— *Change Your Life Without Getting Out of Bed!: The Ultimate Nap Book*. New York: Simon & Schuster, 1999.

———— *The Creative Companion: How to Free Your Creative Spirit*. Berkeley, CA: Celestial Arts Publishing Co., 1991.

———— *Inspiration Sandwich: Stories to Inspire Our Creative Freedom*. Berkeley, CA: Celestial Arts Publishing Co., 1991.

———— *Living Juicy: Daily Morsels for Your Creative Soul*. Berkeley, CA: Celestial Arts Publishing Co., 1991.

———— *Succulent Wild Woman: Dancing with Your Wonder-Full Self*. New York: Simon & Schuster, 1997.

Shaughnessy, Susan. *Walking on Alligators: A Book of Meditations for Writers*. San Francisco: HarperSanFrancisco, 1993.

Toms, Michael, editor. *The Well of Creativity*. Carlsbad, CA: Hay House, 1997.

Ueland, Brenda. *If You Want to Write: A Book About Art, Independence and Spirit*. St. Paul, MN: Graywolf Press, 1997.

Wakefield, Dan. *Creating from the Spirit: A Path to Creative Power in Art and Life*. New York: Ballantine Books, 1996.

Whyte, David. *The Heart Aroused: Poetry and the Preservation of the Soul in Corporate America*. New York: Doubleday, 1994.

Woodman, Marion and Jill Mellick. *Coming Home to Myself*. Berkeley, CA: Conari Press, 1998.

About the Editor

TONA PEARCE MYERS is editorial assistant and production manager at New World Library. She is a published poet who has also contributed to *Mothering* magazine. She received a bachelor's degree in creative writing from Sonoma State University in California. She lives with her husband and son in Novato, California.

If you enjoyed *The Soul of Creativity*, we recommend the following books from New World Library.

Anybody Can Write: A Playful Approach by Roberta Jean Bryant. This book is a fun, user-friendly guide that is filled with great ideas to start you writing and keep you writing. It shows you how to relax and actually have fun writing, and how to discover the richness of your inner resources. It includes effective advice on how to get past the seven common types of writers' blocks. This book will help you finish the project you've been postponing.

Let the Crazy Child Write!: Finding Your Creative Writing Voice by Clive Matson. This book grew out of hundreds of creative writing workshops Clive Matson has led during his career as poet and writer. The book leads readers through a complete series of twelve seminars designed to help them find their creative writing voice. The book is a tool to be used, and readers are encouraged to work with at least one other person and create their own discussion group to work with the material.

Letters to a Young Poet by Rainer Maria Rilke. This luminous translation of Rainer Maria Rilke's classic offers brilliant inspiration to writers, artists, thinkers, and all people who seek to know and express their inner truth. *Letters to a Young Poet* is a classic that should be required reading for everyone who dreams of expressing themselves creatively.

Life — A User's Manual: Great Minds on the Big Questions edited by John Miller. Who am I? What am I doing here? Is there a God? What is life? This inspirational collection of short writings, quotes, and journal excerpts explores the joys, sorrows, and meanings of life — and helps provide some answers.

Wise, profound, surprising, and entertaining, this elegantly produced book will offer instruction, insight, and inspiration to everyone looking for a sense of purpose in life.

Spilling Open: The Art of Becoming Yourself by Sabrina Ward Harrison. The journal pages of a young woman provide an intimate and moving picture of what it means to enter a contemporary adult world filled with contradictions about womanhood. Harrison reveals with tender honesty that in spite of the women's movement, she has more questions than answers about growing up female.

Write from the Heart: Unleashing the Power of Creativity by Hal Zina Bennett. This book presents a revolutionary new approach to writing and the creative spirit. Bennett, author of twenty-five successful books and writing coach to dozens of successful authors, identifies the three key creative resources within each of us, and tells how to access them through writing. Whether you are writing fiction, nonfiction, poetry, or entries in your private journal, this book offers insights into accessing creative resources that you will value for the rest of your life.

NEW WORLD LIBRARY
publishes books and cassettes that inspire
and challenge us to improve the quality
of our lives and the world.

Our books and tapes are available
in bookstores everywhere.
For a catalog of our complete library
of fine books and tapes, contact:

New World Library
14 Pamaron Way
Novato, CA 94949

Phone: (415) 884-2100
Fax: (415) 884-2199
Or call toll free: (800) 972-6657
Catalog requests: Ext. 50
Ordering: Ext. 52

E-mail: escort@nwlib.com
Website: http://www.nwlib.com